*Presented to*

_____

*by*

_____

*on*

_____

# A CHILD'S FIRST
# BIBLE

# A CHILD'S FIRST
# BIBLE

Kenneth N. Taylor

Illustrations by Nadine Wickenden
and Diana Catchpole

Tyndale House Publishers, Inc.
Carol Stream, Illinois

U.S. Creative Director   Jim Bolton
U.S. Editors   Claudia Volkman, Betty Free
U.S. Bible Editor   Dave Barrett

Publisher   Joanna Bicknell
Designers   Peter Bailey and Ann Salisbury
Deputy Art Director   Mark Richards
Publishing Manager   Sarah Phillips

Visit Tyndale's exciting Web site at
www.tyndale.com

*A Child's First Bible*

Text copyright © 2000 by Tyndale House
Foundation

Copyright © 2000 Dorling Kindersley Limited,
London

*TYNDALE* and Tyndale's quill logo are
registered trademarks of Tyndale House
Publishers, Inc.

Published in the Unites States by
Tyndale House Publishers, Inc.
351 Executive Drive
Carol Stream, Illinois 60188

Published in Great Britain by
Dorling Kindersley, London

14 13 12 11 10 09 08
20 19 18 17 16 15 14

ISBN-13: 978-0-8423-3174-6
ISBN-10: 0-8423-3174-3
ISBN-13: 978-0-8423-3199-9 (handled edition)
ISBN-10: 0-8423-3199-9 (handled edition)

Color reproduction by Dot Gradations
Printed and bound in China by
L.Rex Printing Co., Ltd.

Dear Children,

This little book is full of favorite stories from the Bible. It's very important to know these Bible stories, because the Bible is God's book. The Bible tells us how he wants us to live and what he wants us to do.

Why not read one or more of these stories every day? Maybe you can already read. If not, you can ask someone to read the stories to you. At the end of each story, there's a question for you to answer. These questions can help you think about what the story means. After you read a story, you can talk to God. You can tell him that you love him. You can tell him all the things you want him to know.

Remember to ask for God's help every day. Ask him to be with you all the time. Ask him to help you obey him and your parents. And always remember how much God loves you!

Kenneth N. Taylor

In the beginning was only God.

God made the whole world.

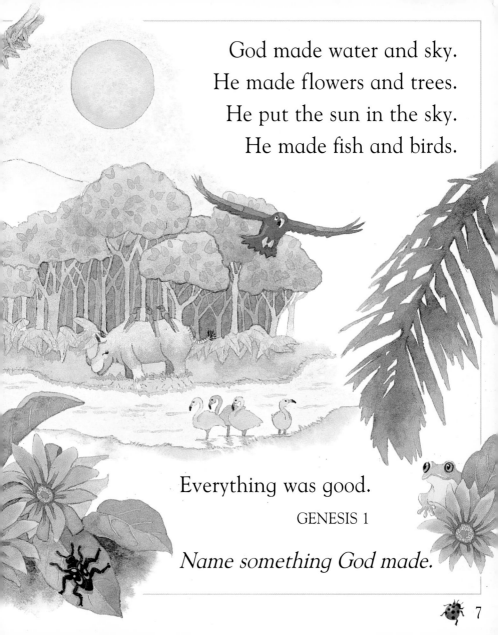

God made water and sky.
He made flowers and trees.
He put the sun in the sky.
He made fish and birds.

Everything was good.

GENESIS 1

*Name something God made.*

7

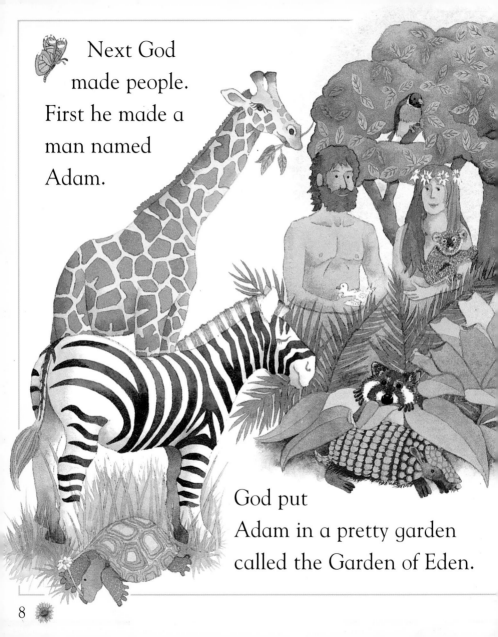

Next God made people. First he made a man named Adam.

God put Adam in a pretty garden called the Garden of Eden.

Angels with a flaming
sword kept them away.

GENESIS 3

Why did Adam and Eve leave the garden?

Cain and Abel were brothers.
Their parents were Adam and Eve.

Abel loved and obeyed God, but
Cain did not. He was angry and
killed Abel. This was very wrong,
and God was very sad. The rest of
Cain's life was hard and difficult.

GENESIS 4

*How did God feel when
Cain didn't obey him?*

God said he would make it rain until there was water everywhere!

Noah believed God.

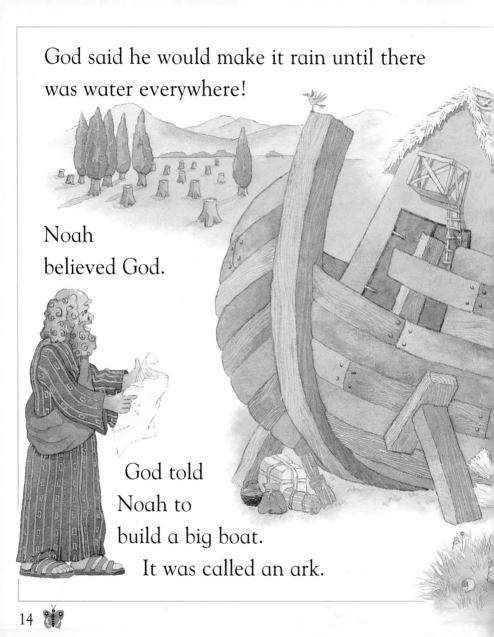

God told Noah to build a big boat. It was called an ark.

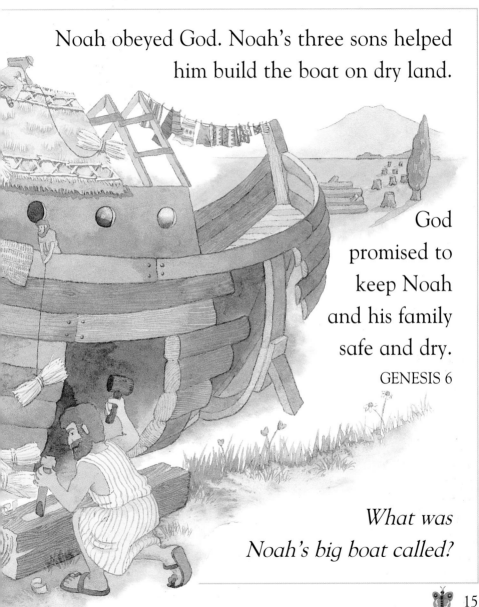

Noah obeyed God. Noah's three sons helped him build the boat on dry land.

God promised to keep Noah and his family safe and dry.

GENESIS 6

*What was Noah's big boat called?*

Finally the big boat was ready.

Then God said, "Noah, take two of each kind of animal and bird with you."

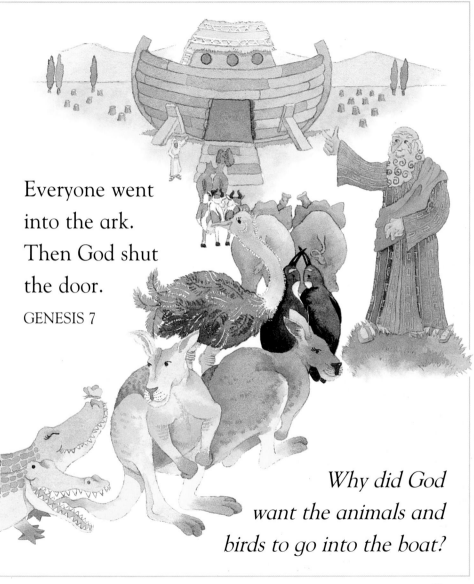

Everyone went
into the ark.
Then God shut
the door.
GENESIS 7

*Why did God
want the animals and
birds to go into the boat?*

17

Noah and his family were safe
inside the ark.

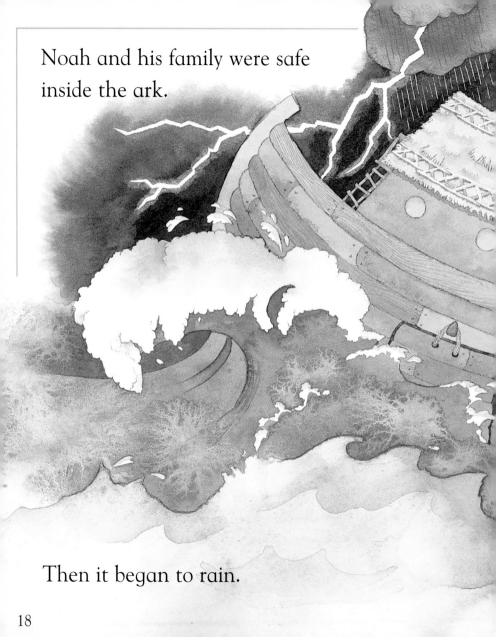

Then it began to rain.

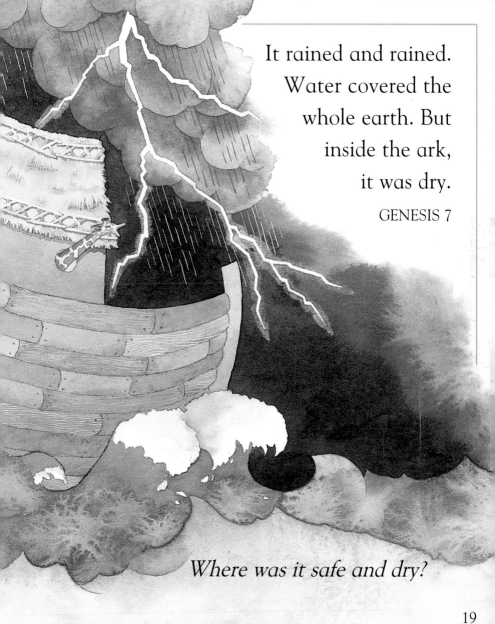

It rained and rained.
Water covered the
whole earth. But
inside the ark,
it was dry.

GENESIS 7

*Where was it safe and dry?*

19

What is all that beautiful color in the sky?
It's a rainbow! God put it there so he
would remember his promise to
never again cover the
world with water.

Noah and his family and the animals came out of the ark. Then Noah thanked God for keeping them safe.

GENESIS 8-9

*Why did God put a rainbow in the sky?*

Some people tried to build a tower
up to the sky. They wanted to
show how great they were.

God was not happy, so he stopped them.
He made them speak different languages.
They couldn't understand each other!
And they couldn't work together
to finish the tower.

GENESIS 11

*Why did the people want to build the tower?*

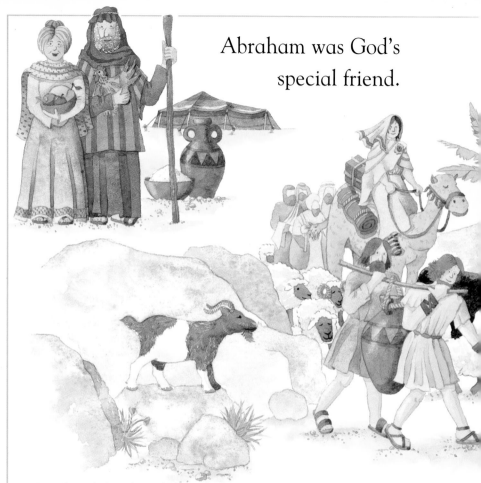

Abraham was God's special friend.

God told Abraham and his wife, Sarah, to move to another country. God promised to do good things for them. Abraham obeyed God.

He knew God would help him,
and he was not afraid. GENESIS 12

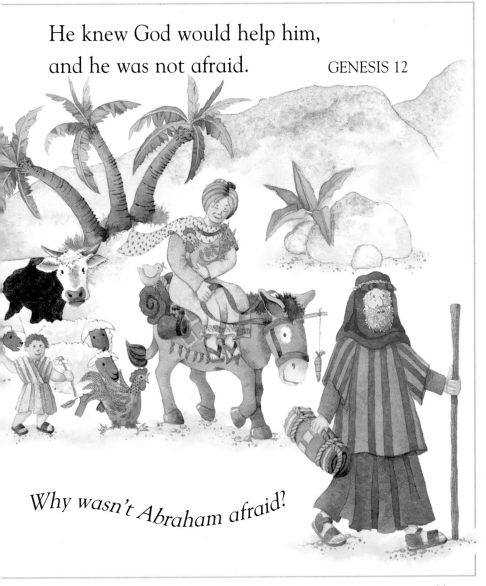

Why wasn't Abraham afraid?

Abraham and his nephew Lot lived near each other. They each owned many cows and sheep.

There wasn't enough grass for all the animals to eat. Abraham told Lot, "We must live in different places."

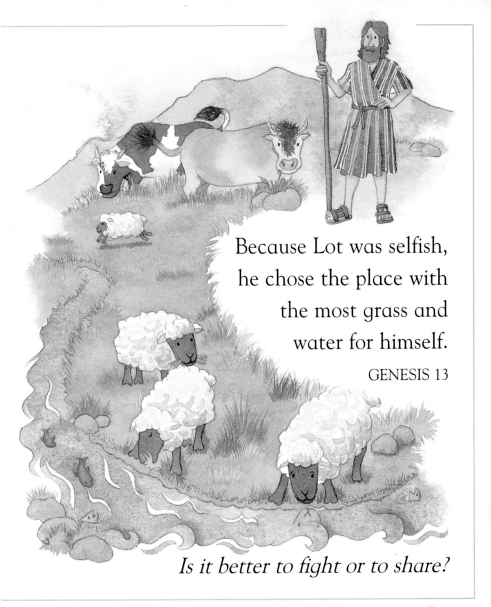

Because Lot was selfish,
he chose the place with
the most grass and
water for himself.

GENESIS 13

*Is it better to fight or to share?*

Sarah and Abraham were sad.
They didn't have any children.

A long time ago God had promised
them a son. Finally, when they were very
old, their baby, Isaac, was born. Then
Abraham and Sarah were very happy!

GENESIS 21

*Is it easy for you to wait
for things you want?*

Isaac grew up
and married
Rebekah. They
had twin sons.

When their son Jacob grew up,
he left home one day. He slept
outside with his head on a rock!

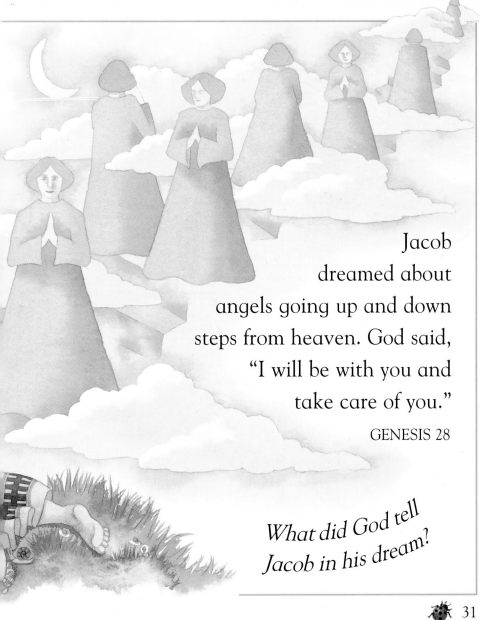

Jacob dreamed about angels going up and down steps from heaven. God said, "I will be with you and take care of you."

GENESIS 28

*What did God tell Jacob in his dream?*

31

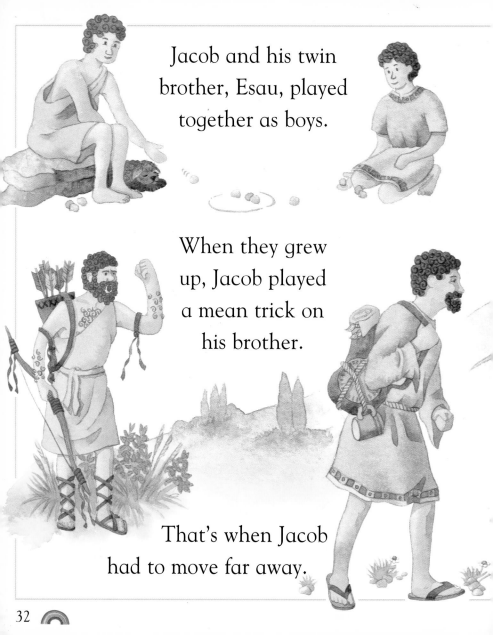

Jacob and his twin brother, Esau, played together as boys.

When they grew up, Jacob played a mean trick on his brother.

That's when Jacob had to move far away.

Many years later, Jacob told Esau he wanted to be friends again. Esau ran to meet Jacob, and they hugged each other!

GENESIS 33

*Did Jacob and Esau become friends again?*

Jacob had twelve sons. One was Joseph.

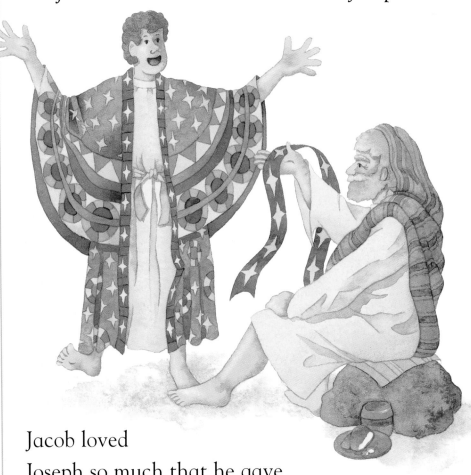

Jacob loved
Joseph so much that he gave
him a special gift. It was a beautiful coat.

Jacob's other sons wanted beautiful coats too.
They became angry with Joseph, and they
were mean to him. GENESIS 37

*Why were Joseph's brothers angry with him?*

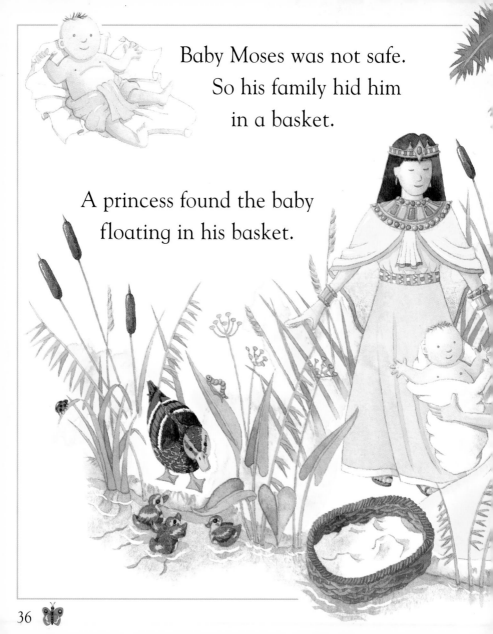

Baby Moses was not safe.
So his family hid him
in a basket.

A princess found the baby
floating in his basket.

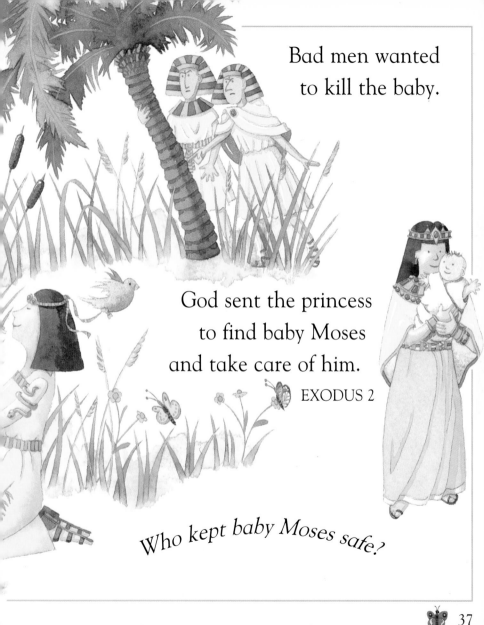

Bad men wanted
to kill the baby.

God sent the princess
to find baby Moses
and take care of him.
EXODUS 2

Who kept baby Moses safe?

37

When Moses grew up, he took care of sheep.

One day he saw a bush on fire, but
the bush didn't burn up! God talked
to Moses from the bush. He said,
"Lead my people out of Egypt."
Moses didn't think he could do it, but
God promised to help him.

EXODUS 3

*What can God help you do?*

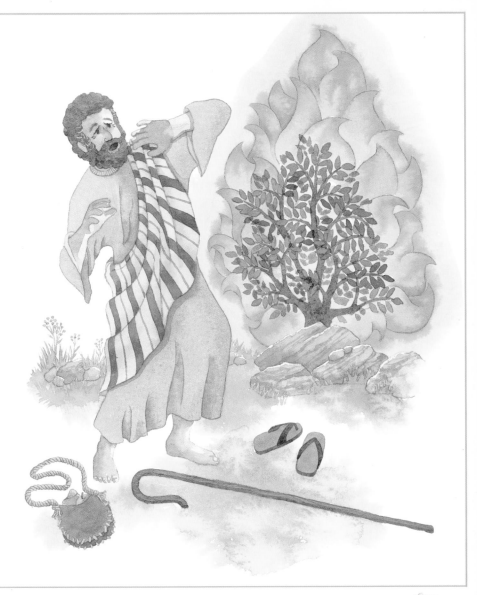

God's people had to make bricks in Egypt.

Pharaoh, the king of Egypt, was very mean. He told his soldiers to whip God's people and make them work even harder. God sent Moses to tell Pharaoh to stop hurting the people.

EXODUS 5

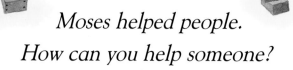

*Moses helped people.*
*How can you help someone?*

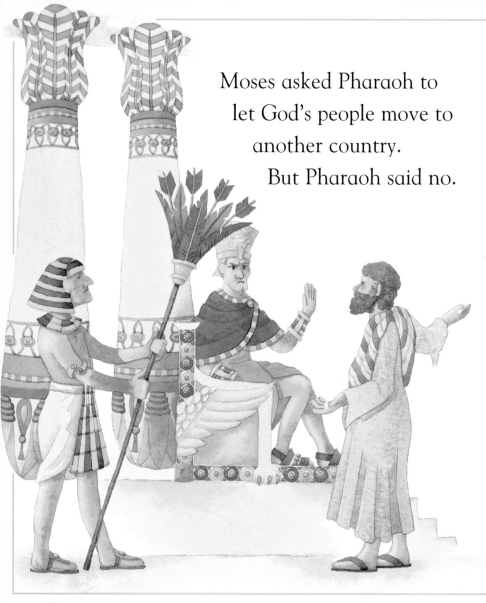

Moses asked Pharaoh to
let God's people move to
another country.
But Pharaoh said no.

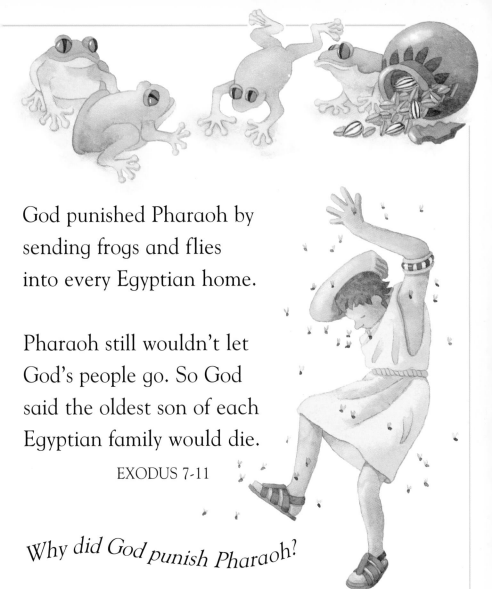

God punished Pharaoh by
sending frogs and flies
into every Egyptian home.

Pharaoh still wouldn't let
God's people go. So God
said the oldest son of each
Egyptian family would die.

EXODUS 7-11

Why did God punish Pharaoh?

Pharaoh still wouldn't listen, so God punished him. But God kept his people safe. Everyone lived who sprinkled lamb's blood on their doors.

The night God did this is called the Passover.

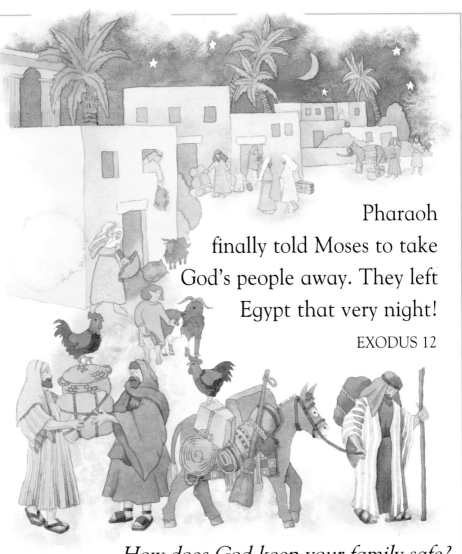

Pharaoh
finally told Moses to take
God's people away. They left
Egypt that very night!

EXODUS 12

*How does God keep your family safe?*

God's people followed Moses to the Red Sea.
They didn't know how to get across it.
God told Moses to hold up his stick.

When he did, God made a path through
the water so the people could walk
across on dry ground. They were safe!

EXODUS 14

*How did God help his people?*

God's people could not find any food.

They were very hungry.
God sent them little pieces
of bread from heaven.

Every morning he sent enough for that day.

EXODUS 16

*What does God give you to eat?*

God's people came to a place where there was no water to drink.

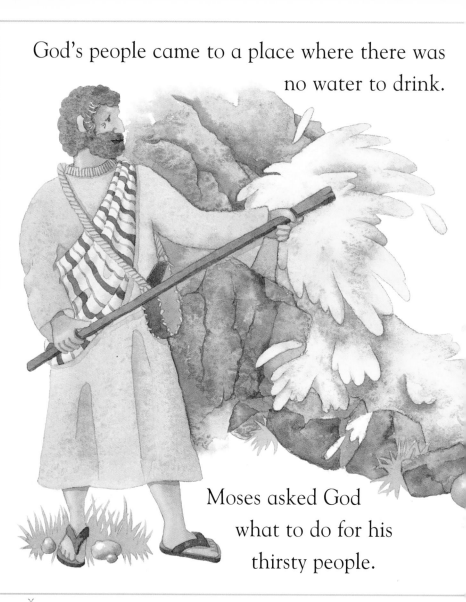

Moses asked God what to do for his thirsty people.

God told him to hit a big rock with his stick.
When Moses did, water came out, and there
was enough for everyone!

EXODUS 17

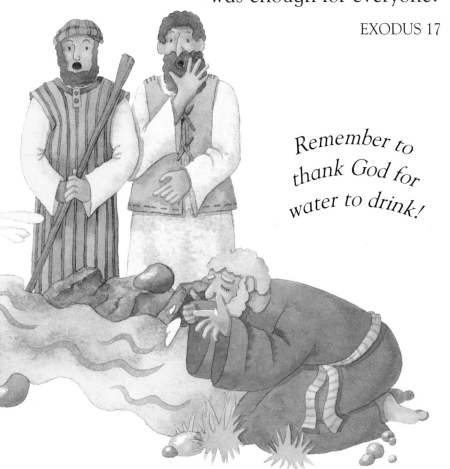

Remember to thank God for water to drink!

51

An army came to fight God's people.

As long as Moses raised his special stick toward heaven, God's people would win. But his arms got tired. So Moses' brother and a friend helped him.

They found a stone for him to sit on.
They held his arms up until the sun went down.
And God's people won the battle.

EXODUS 17

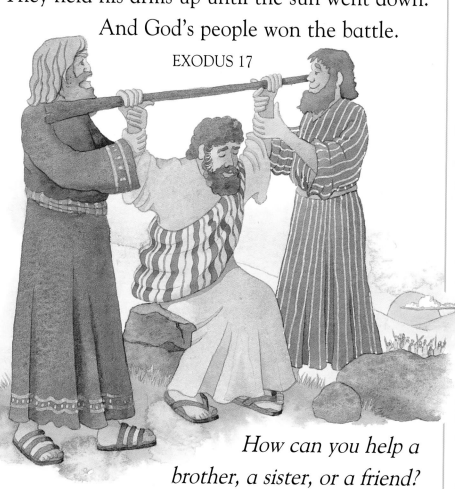

*How can you help a
brother, a sister, or a friend?*

53

Moses climbed up a big mountain. There God gave him ten special rules on two stones. God wanted his people to know how to obey him.

One rule is to love God. Another rule is to love and obey your parents. We call these the Ten Commandments.

EXODUS 20, 24

*What are God's rules called?*

While Moses was on the mountain with God, Aaron made a calf. He made it from the gold jewelry everyone brought him.

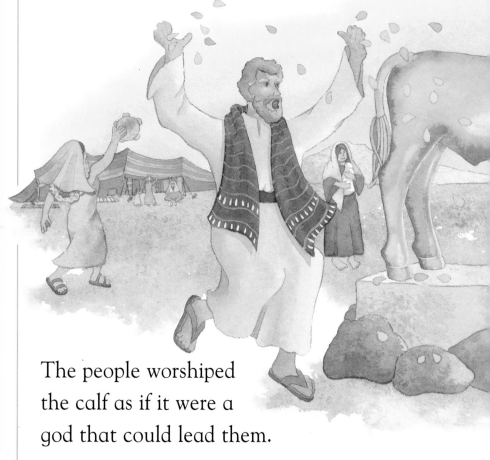

The people worshiped the calf as if it were a god that could lead them.

This made God angry. But Moses asked God to forgive them. And God did.

EXODUS 32

Why was God angry with the people?

Moses gave the people God's directions for making a tabernacle. This was a special tent where God's people could worship him. Everyone worked hard until it was finished.

EXODUS 35-36

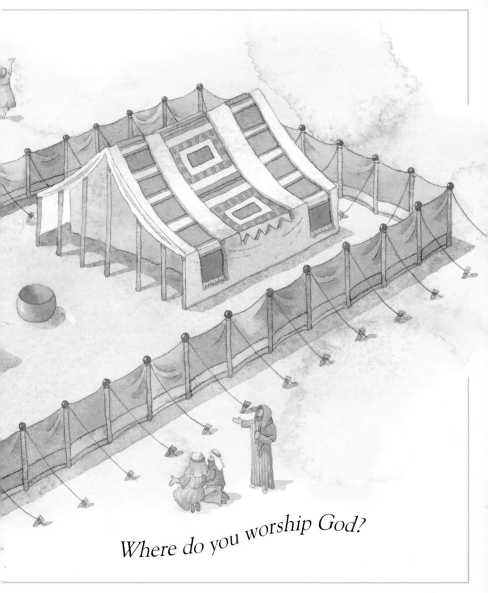

*Where do you worship God?*

The people moved to
new places many times
in the wilderness.

They moved on whenever
a special cloud above the
tabernacle moved.

God was in the cloud,
and the people
followed him.

EXODUS 40

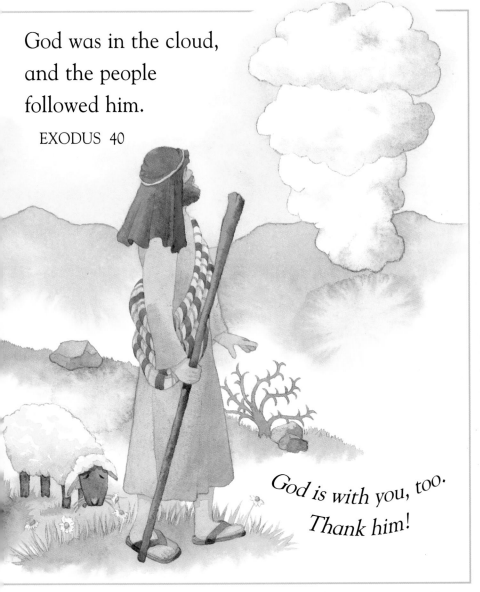

*God is with you, too.*
*Thank him!*

Moses sent twelve men to see the
land God promised to give his people.

Joshua and Caleb came back to tell
everyone what a beautiful country it was.
The other ten men were scared of the
giants who lived there. But Joshua and
Caleb knew God would take care of
them no matter what.

NUMBERS 13-14

*When you're afraid, what can you do?*

God's people were afraid. Poisonous snakes
were biting some of them.

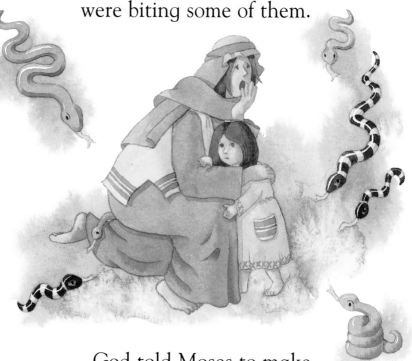

God told Moses to make
a metal snake and put it on top of a pole.
People with snakebites could look at the
metal snake. Then God would heal them.

NUMBERS 21

*When you are sick, who can make you well?*

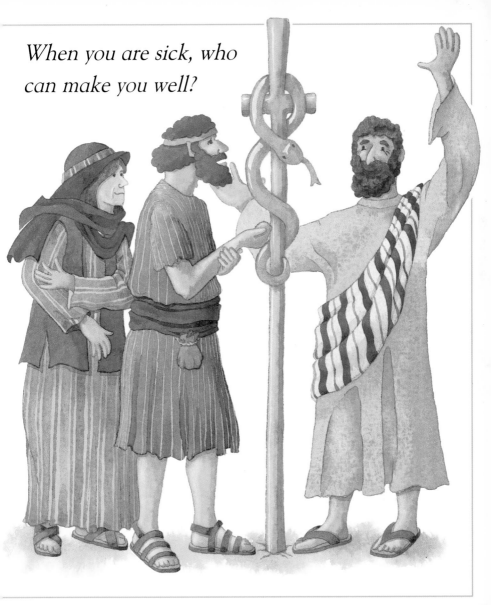

Balaam was taking a trip. God sent an angel with a sword to stop him. Balaam's donkey saw the angel and wouldn't move.

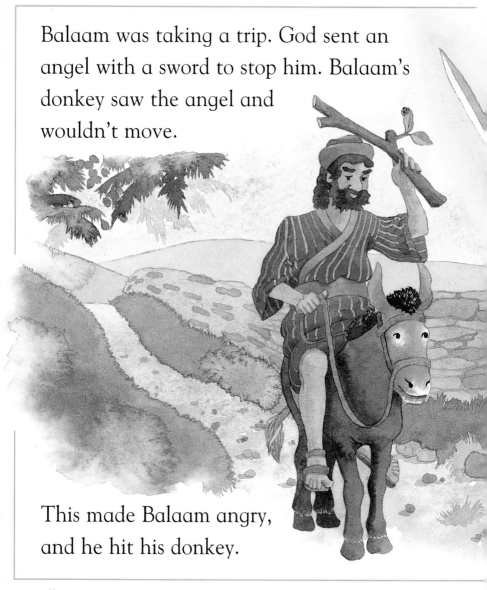

This made Balaam angry, and he hit his donkey.

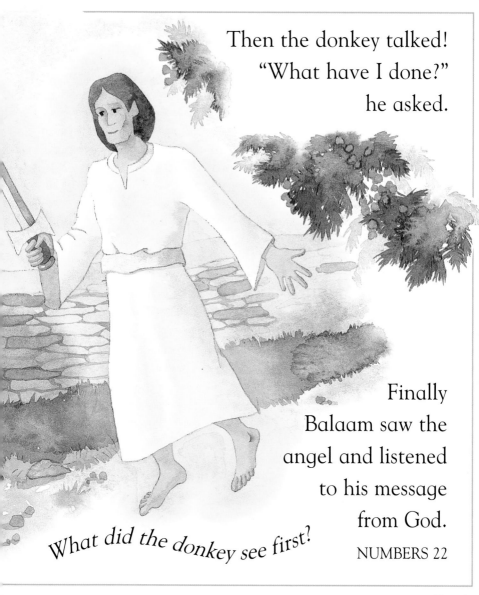

Then the donkey talked!
"What have I done?"
he asked.

Finally
Balaam saw the
angel and listened
to his message
from God.

NUMBERS 22

What did the donkey see first?

67

After Moses died, God made Joshua the new leader. He had to help God's people cross the Jordan River.

Joshua told the men who carried the special box with God's laws inside to go first.

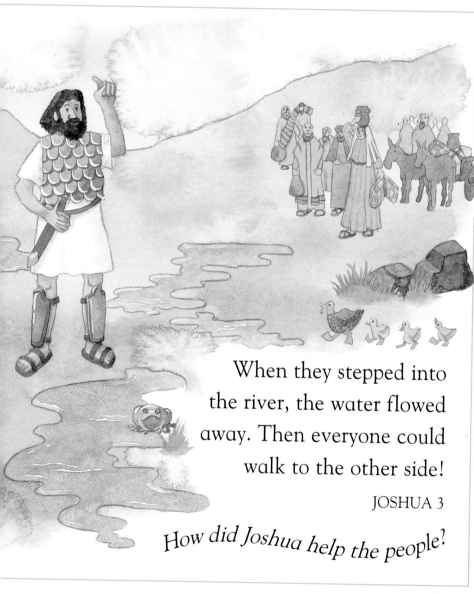

When they stepped into the river, the water flowed away. Then everyone could walk to the other side!

JOSHUA 3

How did Joshua help the people?

Joshua was the new leader of God's people.
Their enemies would not let
them into the city of Jericho.
But God showed Joshua a way.

Joshua and the people
marched around the walls of the city.
They blew their horns and shouted.

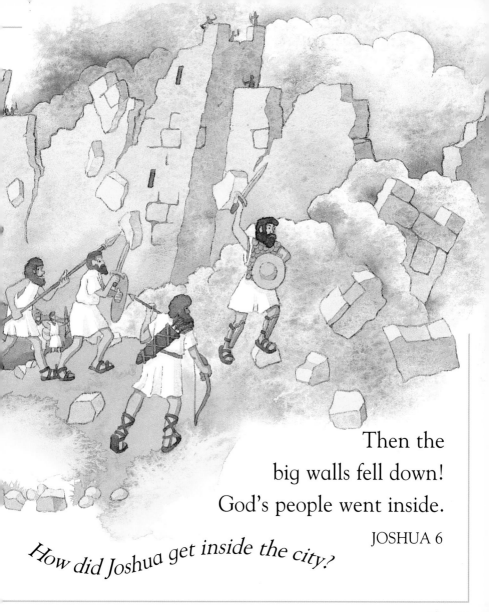

Then the
big walls fell down!
God's people went inside.

JOSHUA 6

How did Joshua get inside the city?

Five armies came to fight Joshua
and God's people.

Joshua's army was winning.
But they needed more time.
So Joshua prayed, "Let the
sun stand still."

And God stopped the sun right in the middle
of the sky! It didn't go down for a long time.

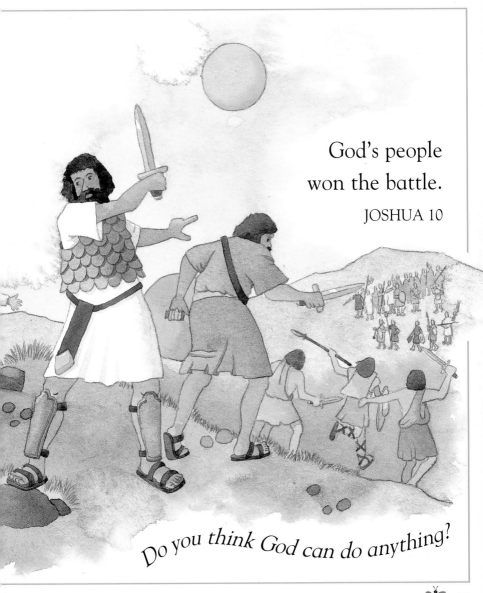

God's people
won the battle.

JOSHUA 10

Do you *think* God can do anything?

73

Thousands of men were waiting to fight the enemies of God's people. God told Gideon that his army should be small.

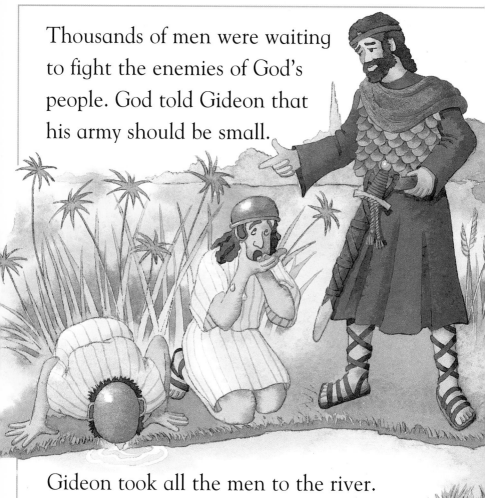

Gideon took all the men to the river. God said only the 300 men who drank from their hands could be in the army.

Bravely Gideon took only these men, and
God helped them win the fight!          JUDGES 7

*Will you let God help you be brave?*

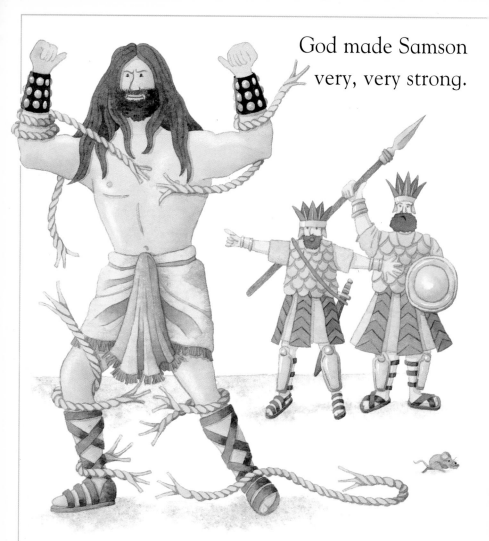

God made Samson very, very strong.

He broke the ropes that tied him!

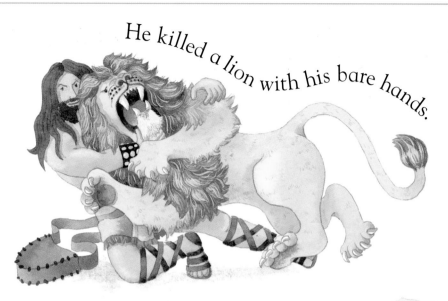

*He killed a lion with his bare hands.*

He knocked down a large building. It fell on many of God's enemies.

JUDGES 14-16

*Who made Samson strong?*

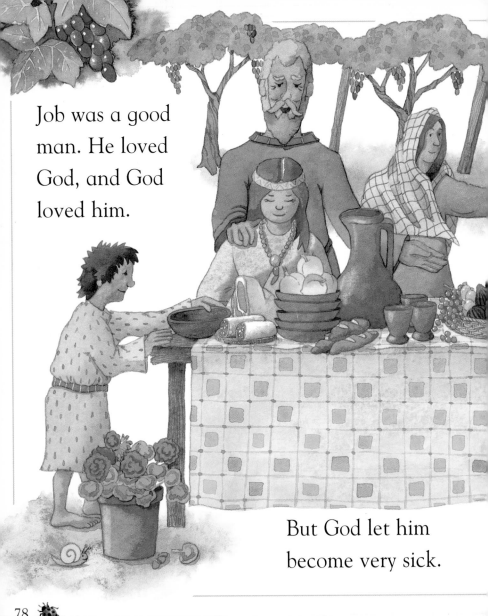

Job was a good
man. He loved
God, and God
loved him.

But God let him
become very sick.

He hurt all over.

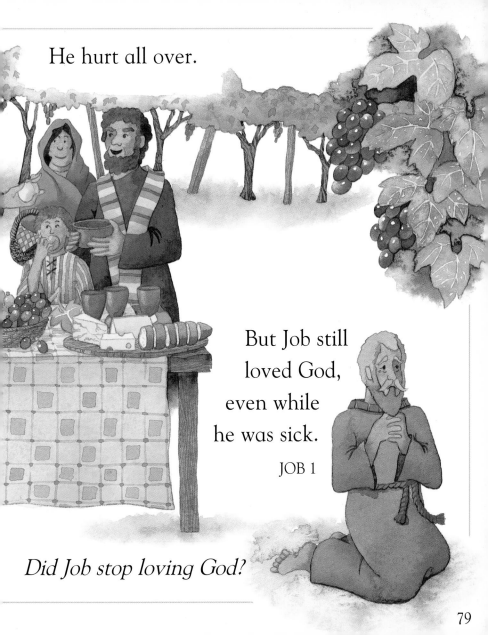

But Job still
loved God,
even while
he was sick.

JOB 1

*Did Job stop loving God?*

79

Naomi was very sad because her husband and two sons had died.

Ruth went with Naomi on a long trip to help her. Then God blessed both of them. God was pleased because Ruth was kind to Naomi.

RUTH 1

*Name something kind you can do for someone in your family.*

Samuel was Eli's helper.

One night when Samuel was sleeping,
God called to him. "Samuel! Samuel!"
The boy thought Eli was calling him.

Finally Samuel knew God was calling him.
Samuel answered, "Tell me what you want,
and I will do it." 1 SAMUEL 2

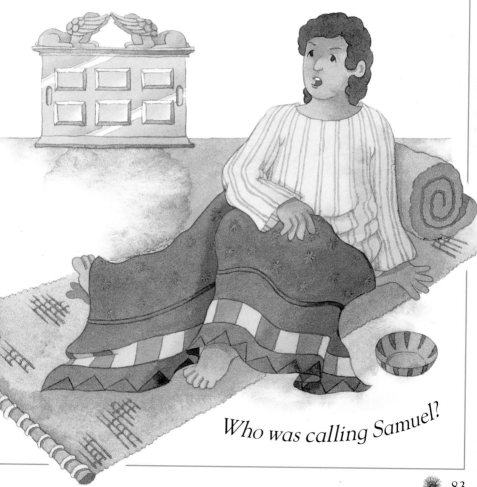

*Who was calling Samuel?*

83

God chose Saul to be the king of God's people.
Saul was strong and good-looking.
But he didn't love God.
Saul did things that were wrong.

So God said he couldn't
be king anymore.      1 SAMUEL 8

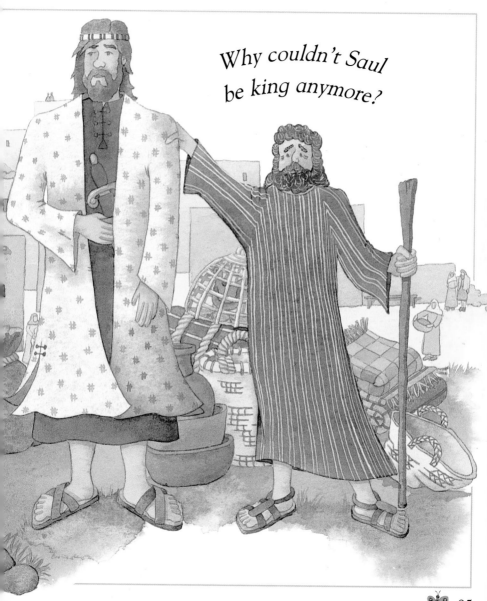

Why couldn't Saul
be king anymore?

85

David took care of his father's sheep.

He led them to
the best grass for the sheep to eat.

And David kept the sheep safe from wild animals like lions and bears. David was a good shepherd.

1 SAMUEL 16

What made David a good shepherd?

One day a lion tried to catch one of David's sheep and eat it. David grabbed the sheep away from the lion.

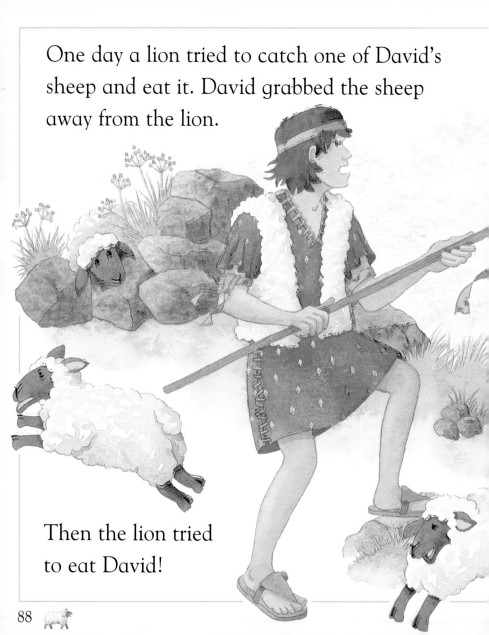

Then the lion tried to eat David!

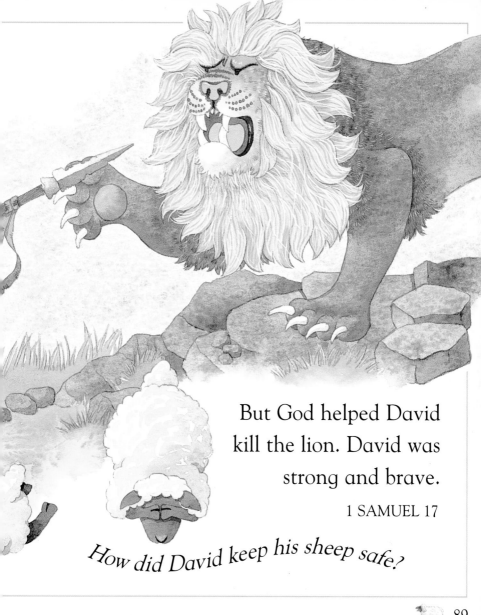

But God helped David
kill the lion. David was
strong and brave.

1 SAMUEL 17

*How did David keep his sheep safe?*

89

Goliath was one of God's enemies. He was nine feet tall! He said he would kill anyone who dared to come and fight him.

David wasn't afraid of Goliath because he knew God was on his side.

David used
his slingshot
and a stone.

The stone
hit Goliath
between the eyes
and killed him!

1 SAMUEL 17

*Why wasn't
David afraid?*

91

After David killed Goliath,
everyone praised him for
being so brave.

One of his new friends was
Jonathan, the king's son. Jonathan
liked David so much that he gave
him his robe and his sword. David
and Jonathan were best friends.

1 SAMUEL 18

*Do you have a best friend?*

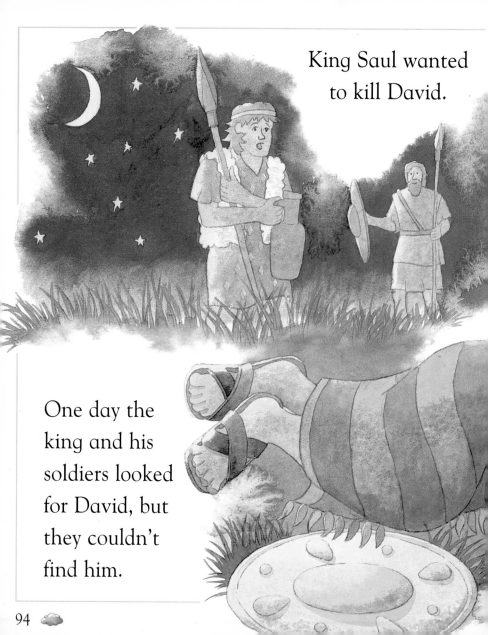

King Saul wanted
to kill David.

One day the
king and his
soldiers looked
for David, but
they couldn't
find him.

That night, while the king was sleeping, David came and took his spear. But David didn't hurt him, because God had chosen Saul to be king.

1 SAMUEL 26

Why didn't David hurt the king?

One day when David was taking
care of his father's sheep,
Samuel sent for him. When
David came, he saw his
father and brothers.

Samuel was talking to them.
Samuel said that God wanted
David to be the new king!

What a surprise to David
and his family!

1 SAMUEL 16

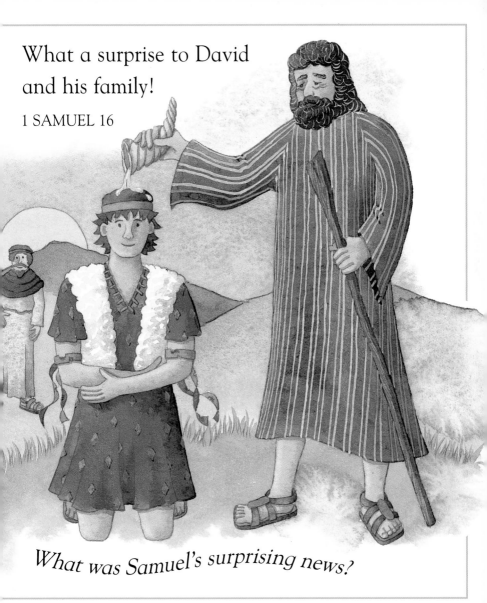

*What was Samuel's surprising news?*

King Saul was killed in battle.
Then David became the new king.

He wanted the box with God's rules
inside to be near him. So some men
carried the special box into the city of
Jerusalem. As they did, David and all
the people celebrated with lots of
singing and dancing.

2 SAMUEL 6

*Do you have a Bible?*
*Then God's rules are near you!*

One day King David saw a beautiful young woman. She was taking a bath in a pool near his palace. David wanted her for himself, so he did a terrible thing.

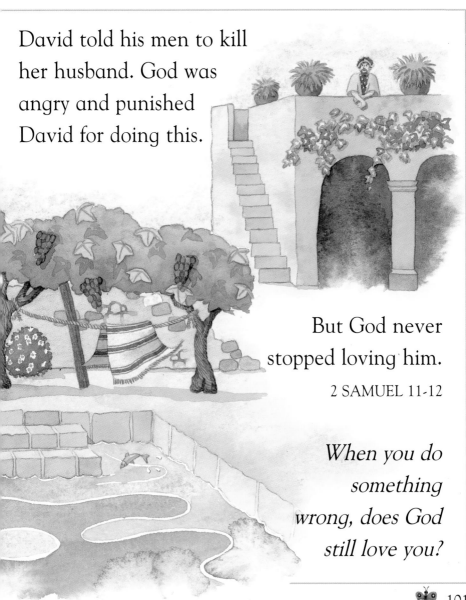

David told his men to kill her husband. God was angry and punished David for doing this.

But God never stopped loving him.

2 SAMUEL 11-12

*When you do something wrong, does God still love you?*

101

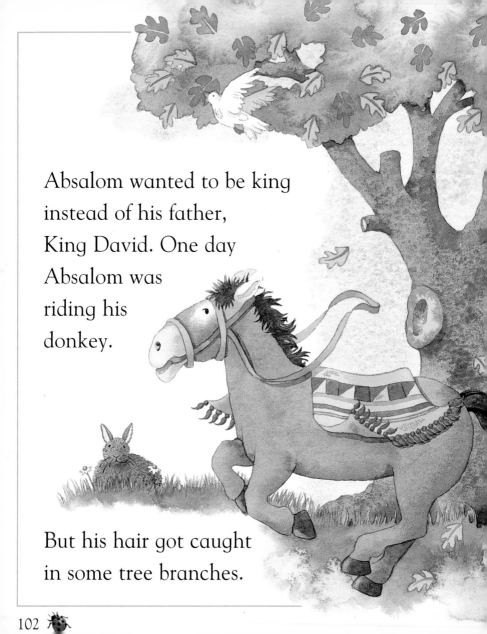

Absalom wanted to be king
instead of his father,
King David. One day
Absalom was
riding his
donkey.

But his hair got caught
in some tree branches.

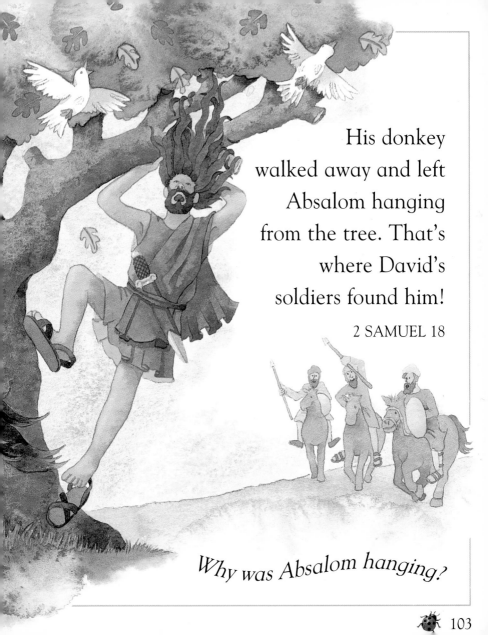

His donkey walked away and left Absalom hanging from the tree. That's where David's soldiers found him!

2 SAMUEL 18

*Why was Absalom hanging?*

103

Solomon was King David's son.
He rode on the king's mule.

David told him to do this so people
would know that Solomon was their
new king. One of God's helpers poured
oil on Solomon's head to show that
God was pleased. Many people played
happy music. They prayed that King
Solomon would live for a long time.

1 KINGS 1

*Why did Solomon ride on King David's mule?*

Solomon asked God to help him be a good king. So God made him very wise.

One day two women came to the king. Each of them wanted the same baby. Solomon was wise.

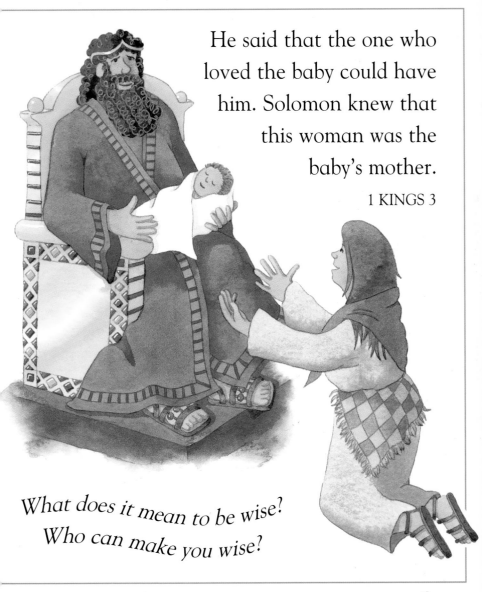

He said that the one who loved the baby could have him. Solomon knew that this woman was the baby's mother.

1 KINGS 3

What does it mean to be wise?
Who can make you wise?

King Solomon built a temple. It was a beautiful building where people worshiped God.

Solomon talked to God there. He thanked God and praised him because God is so great and good.

Solomon asked God to always listen to his prayers and answer them.

1 KINGS 6, 8

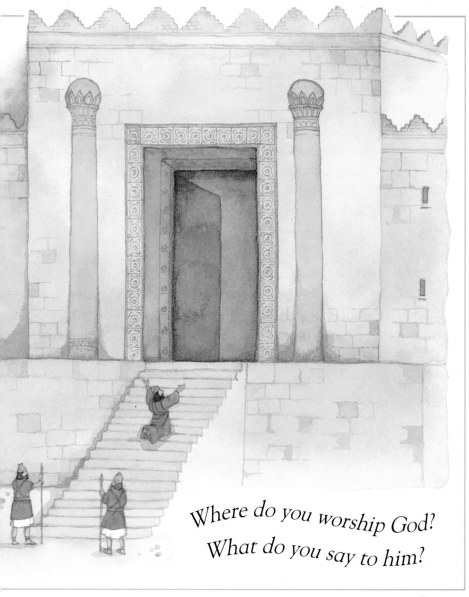

*Where do you worship God?*
*What do you say to him?*

Solomon was a good king as long as he obeyed God. But Solomon began praying to animals made of gold and silver and even stone!

Could these fake gods answer his prayers? Of course not. Our real God was angry because Solomon did this. He said he would give Solomon's kingdom to somebody else.

1 KINGS 11

*Why was God angry with Solomon?*

Elijah was God's helper. Elijah told the king it would not rain for a long time because of the bad things the king was doing.

God wanted Elijah to be safe. He told him where he could go to hide from the king. Elijah would find water to drink there.

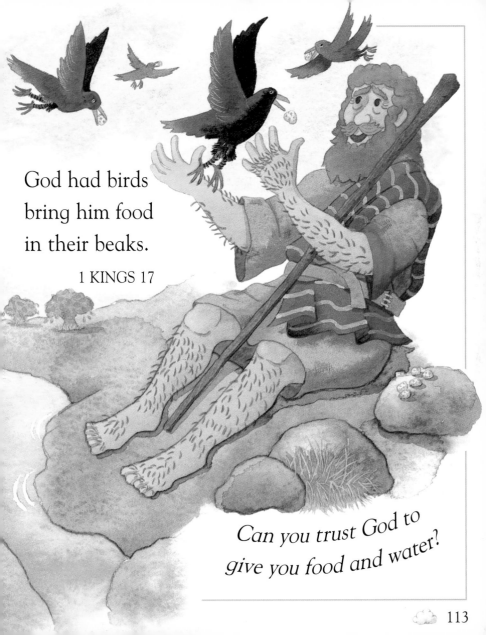

God had birds
bring him food
in their beaks.

1 KINGS 17

*Can you trust God to
give you food and water?*

113

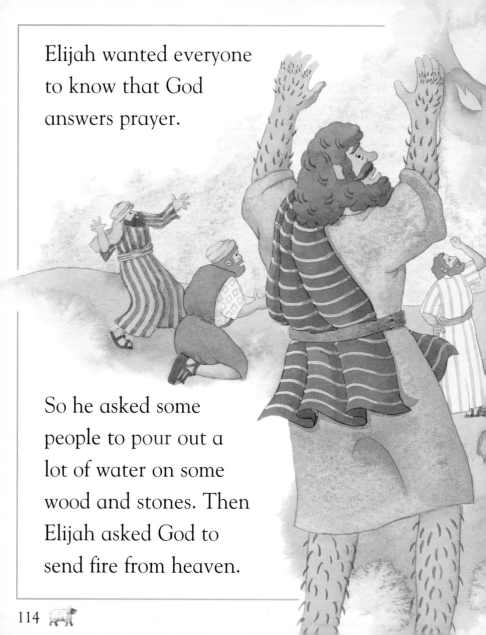

Elijah wanted everyone to know that God answers prayer.

So he asked some people to pour out a lot of water on some wood and stones. Then Elijah asked God to send fire from heaven.

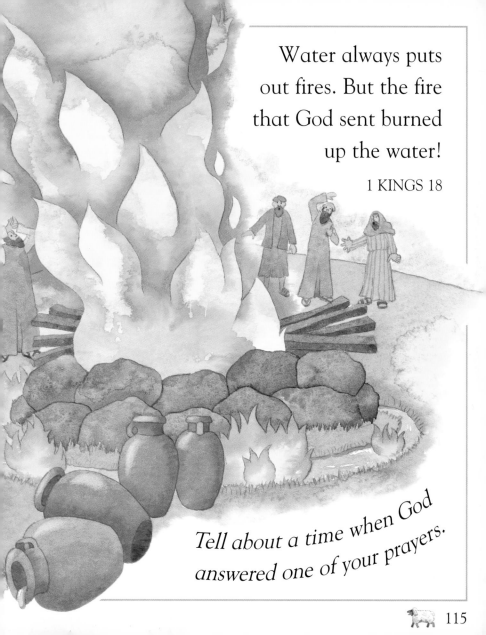

Water always puts
out fires. But the fire
that God sent burned
up the water!

1 KINGS 18

*Tell about a time when God
answered one of your prayers.*

115

God wanted Elijah to live with him
in heaven forever. So God sent
horses made of fire to
bring Elijah to him.

They were pulling a
wagon called a chariot.
It was made of fire, too.
Elijah rode in the chariot
all the way up to heaven!

Elisha, who was God's new
helper, watched him go.

2 KINGS 2

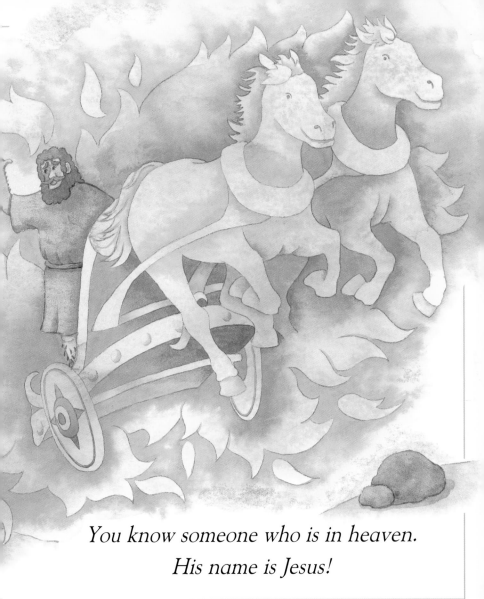

*You know someone who is in heaven.*
*His name is Jesus!*

A woman with two sons had no money, but she had a jar of cooking oil.

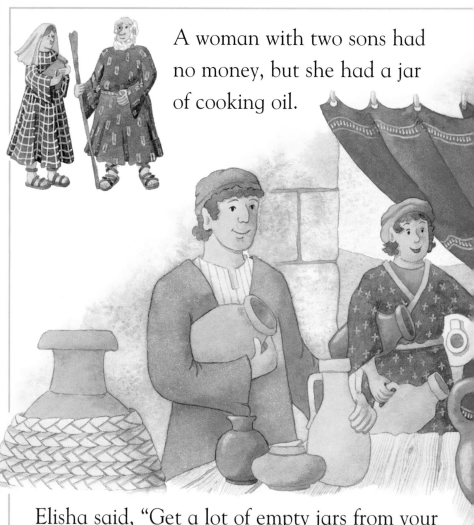

Elisha said, "Get a lot of empty jars from your friends. Fill the jars with oil from your jar."

The woman poured and poured the oil from her jar. But no matter how much oil she poured, God kept her jar full of oil!

Elisha told the woman to sell the oil so she would have plenty of money.

2 KINGS 4

*It was God who showed Elisha how to help. Who can help your family?*

Elisha often walked from town to town so he could be God's helper in different places.

A man and woman in one town always let him stay at their house. One day their son died. But when Elisha prayed, God made the boy come back to life!

2 KINGS 4

*Is there anything that God can't do?*

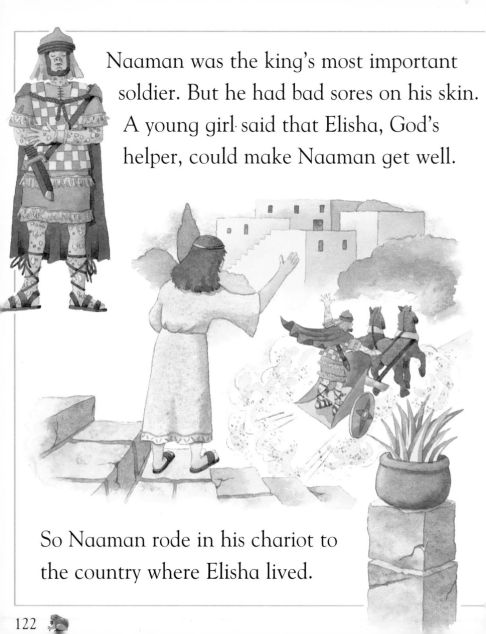

Naaman was the king's most important soldier. But he had bad sores on his skin. A young girl said that Elisha, God's helper, could make Naaman get well.

So Naaman rode in his chariot to the country where Elisha lived.

Elisha told Naaman to wash in the Jordan River seven times. As soon as he did it, God healed him!

2 KINGS 5

*Tell about a time when you were sick and God showed a doctor how to help you.*

123

King Joash wanted
God's house to be
beautiful.

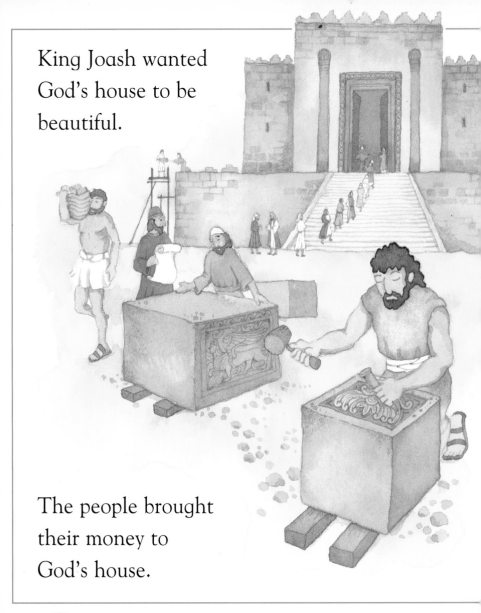

The people brought
their money to
God's house.

The money was used to buy wood and stones.

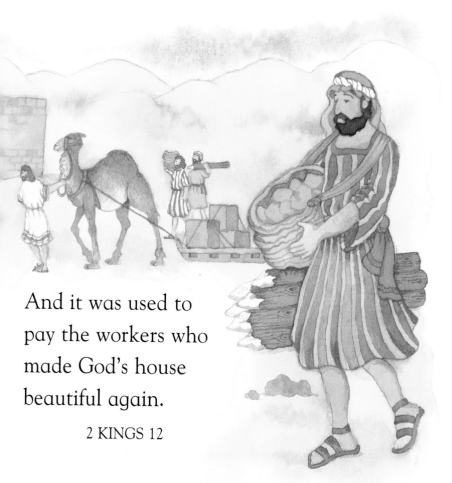

And it was used to
pay the workers who
made God's house
beautiful again.

2 KINGS 12

*Will you give some of your money to God?*

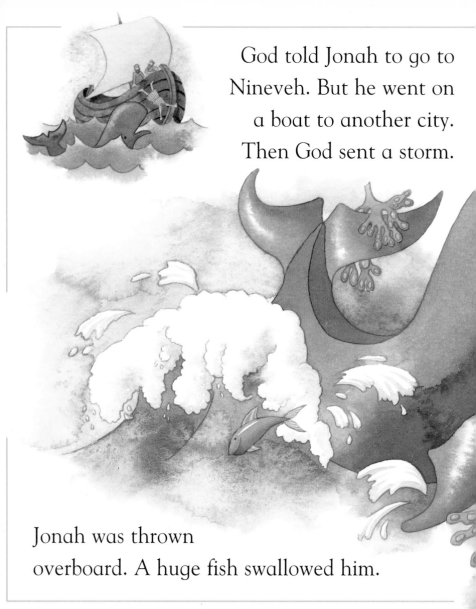

God told Jonah to go to
Nineveh. But he went on
a boat to another city.
Then God sent a storm.

Jonah was thrown
overboard. A huge fish swallowed him.

After three days the fish coughed him out.
Then Jonah went where God told him to go.

JONAH 1-2

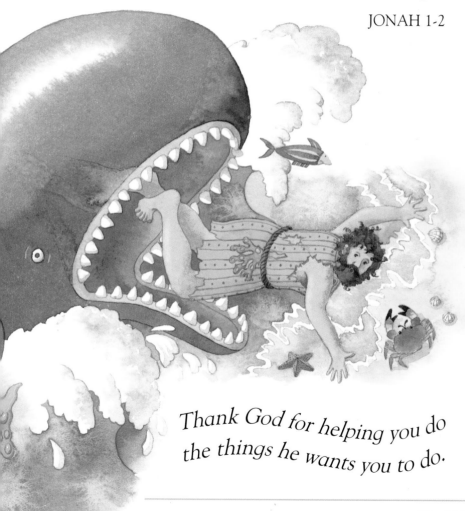

Thank God for helping you do
the things he wants you to do.

Hezekiah was a very good king.
He always obeyed God.
Other kings had worshiped big
gold idols that looked like
people or animals.

King Hezekiah and his helpers
smashed the idols. The king knew
that these were just fake gods.

2 KINGS 18

*What made Hezekiah a good king?*

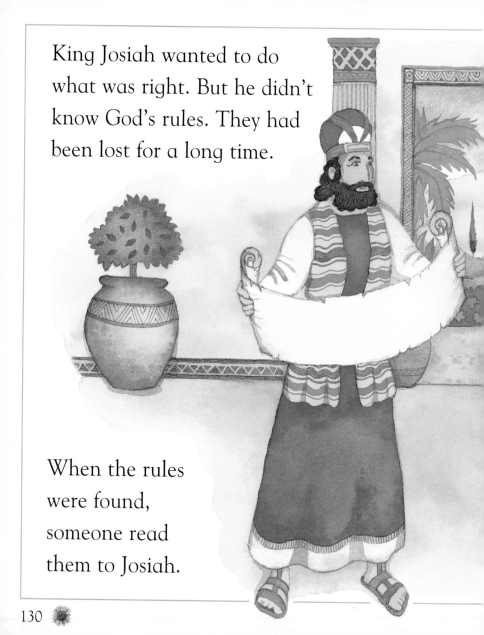

King Josiah wanted to do what was right. But he didn't know God's rules. They had been lost for a long time.

When the rules were found, someone read them to Josiah.

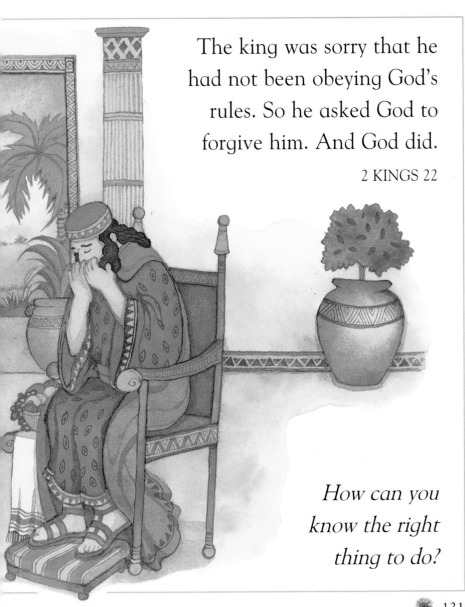

The king was sorry that he had not been obeying God's rules. So he asked God to forgive him. And God did.

2 KINGS 22

*How can you know the right thing to do?*

131

Jeremiah gave people messages from God. The people did not want to listen to Jeremiah.

Some men threw him into a deep hole so he couldn't give more of God's messages.

But the king told his men to get Jeremiah out.

JEREMIAH 38

How did God take care of Jeremiah?

Daniel and his three friends were living in a country far away from their homes.

They loved God and always wanted to obey him. So God made them wise.

They gave good advice to the king. They could always tell him the best thing to do.

DANIEL 1

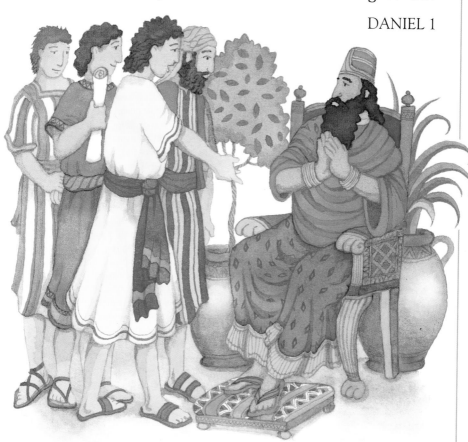

Who can make you wise?

The king ordered his people to make a giant statue that looked like him. He said everyone had to bow down and worship it.

Daniel's three friends wouldn't do it. They said they would worship only God, no matter what the king would do to them.

DANIEL 3

*Why wouldn't Daniel's friends do what the king said?*

The king heard that Shadrach, Meshach, and Abednego would not worship his gold statue.

So he gave orders to throw them into a very hot fire.

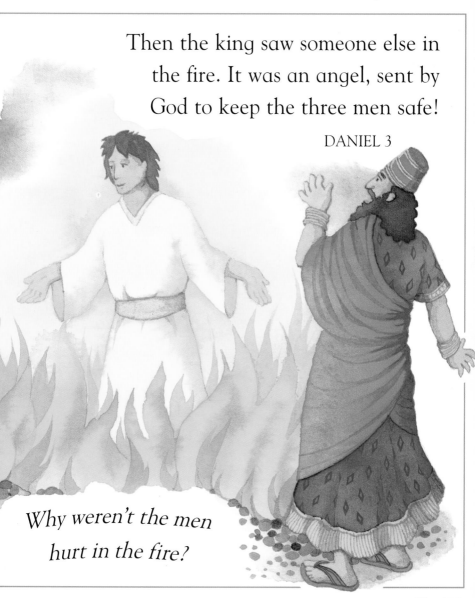

Then the king saw someone else in the fire. It was an angel, sent by God to keep the three men safe!

DANIEL 3

*Why weren't the men hurt in the fire?*

One night the king was giving a big party.
Suddenly everyone saw a hand writing
some words on the wall.

The king was afraid. He asked Daniel
what the words meant. Daniel said it
was a message from God, telling him
he could no longer be king.

DANIEL 5

*Why was the king afraid?*

Daniel loved praying to God. But the king said, "Don't pray to God. Pray to me instead!" Daniel knew this was wrong, so he kept praying only to God.

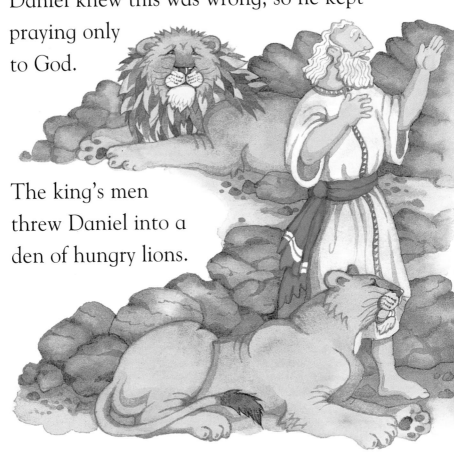

The king's men threw Daniel into a den of hungry lions.

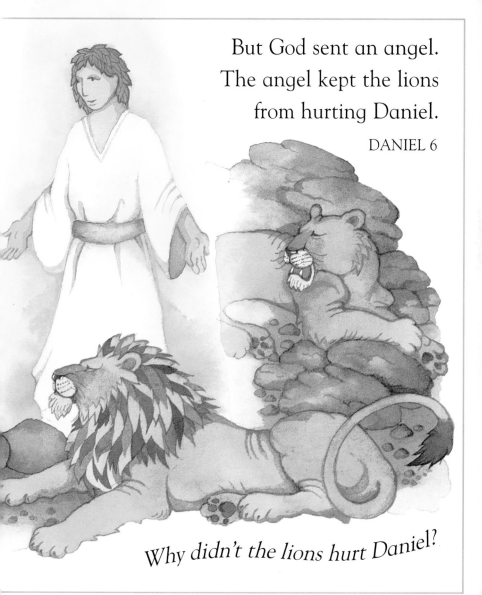

But God sent an angel.
The angel kept the lions
from hurting Daniel.

DANIEL 6

Why didn't the lions hurt Daniel?

Esther was a beautiful queen.
She was Jewish, but the king
didn't know that. He signed a law
for all Jewish people to be killed.

Queen Esther was afraid, but she
was brave. She asked the king to
save her people. So the king signed
a new law to help the Jews.

ESTHER 5-8

*Why did the king decide to
help the Jewish people?*

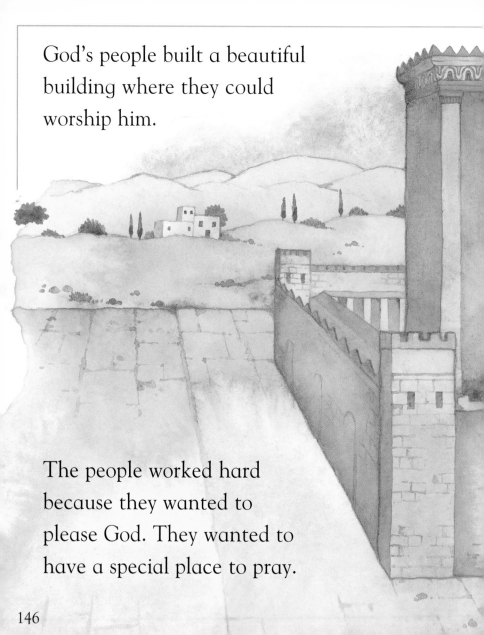

God's people built a beautiful building where they could worship him.

The people worked hard because they wanted to please God. They wanted to have a special place to pray.

146

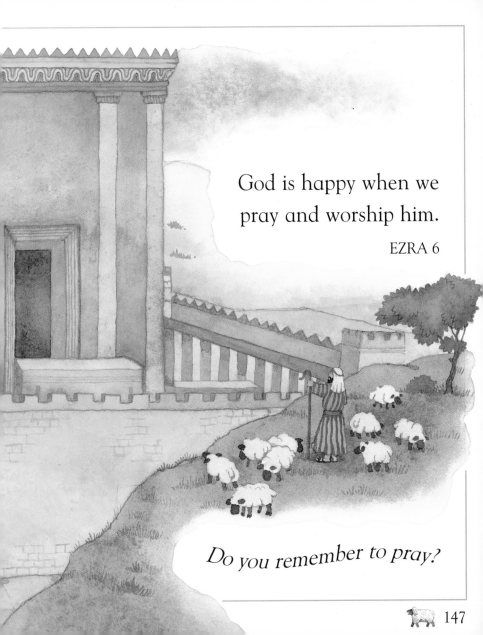

God is happy when we pray and worship him.

EZRA 6

Do you remember to pray?

147

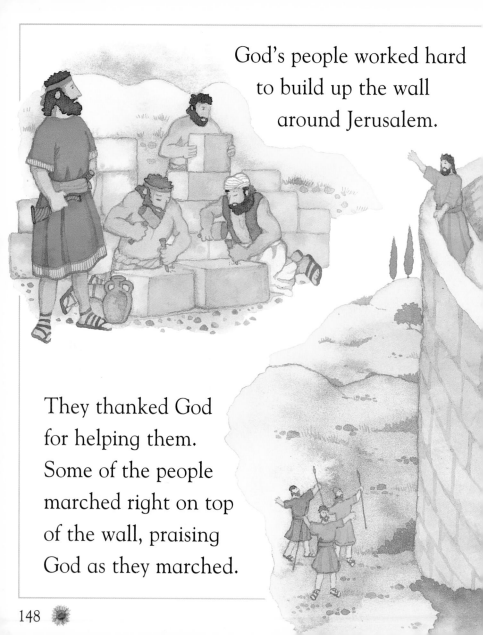

God's people worked hard to build up the wall around Jerusalem.

They thanked God for helping them. Some of the people marched right on top of the wall, praising God as they marched.

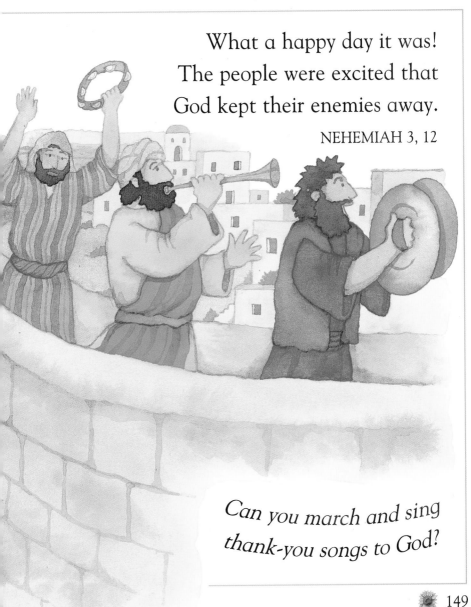

What a happy day it was!
The people were excited that
God kept their enemies away.

NEHEMIAH 3, 12

*Can you march and sing
thank-you songs to God?*

149

God sent the angel Gabriel to tell
Mary something very important.

At first Mary was afraid. But the angel
said, "God wants you to be the mother
of his Son, Jesus!" Mary said she would
do whatever God wanted. She was
very happy to become Jesus' mother.

LUKE 1

*Will you do whatever God wants you to do?*

Zechariah and Elizabeth were very old when they had a baby boy.

Zechariah knew he would call the baby John because that's what an angel told him to do.

God helped Zechariah know that his son would tell many people about Jesus when he grew up.

LUKE 1

What can you tell people about Jesus?

Mary and Joseph came to the town of Bethlehem.

The inn was full, so they stayed in a stable with the animals. God's Son was born that night. Mary named her baby Jesus.

LUKE 2

Sing a song to Jesus!

155

On the night Jesus was born, some shepherds were taking care of their sheep. An angel came to tell them that they could find baby Jesus in a manger.

Suddenly thousands of angels appeared in the sky.

They praised God for sending Jesus to be our Savior.

LUKE 2

You can thank God for Jesus too!

When the angels left, the shepherds said, "Let's go to Bethlehem. Let's see if we can find this baby."

They found Jesus lying in a manger, just as the angel had said. How excited they were! They told everyone the good news. They praised God all the way back to their fields.

LUKE 2

*You can tell everyone about Jesus' birth too!*

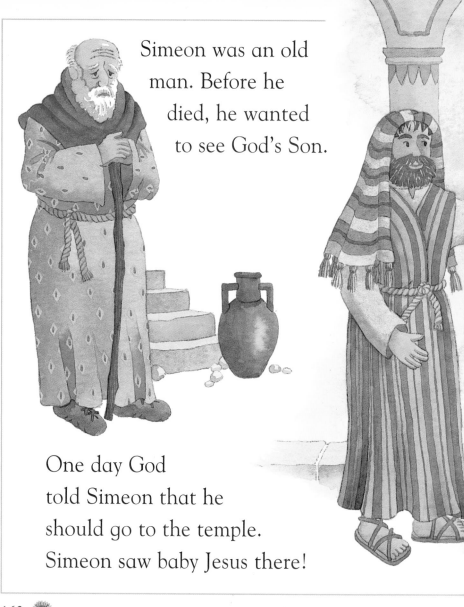

Simeon was an old man. Before he died, he wanted to see God's Son.

One day God told Simeon that he should go to the temple. Simeon saw baby Jesus there!

Simeon held God's little Son in his arms and thanked God for him.

LUKE 2

*Whose Son is Jesus?*

161

Some wise men followed a special star in the sky. It led them to the house where the little boy Jesus lived.

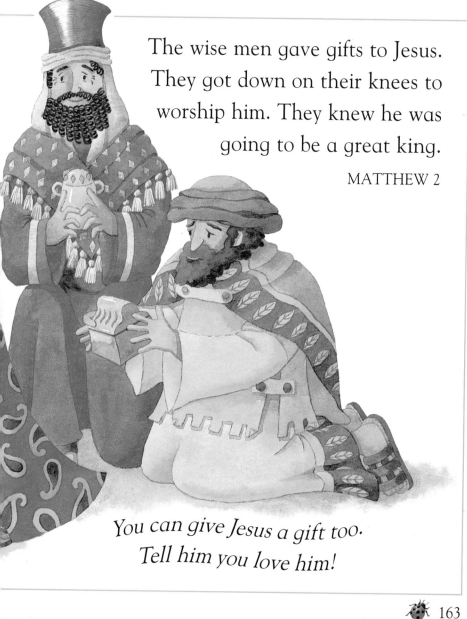

The wise men gave gifts to Jesus.
They got down on their knees to
worship him. They knew he was
going to be a great king.

MATTHEW 2

You can give Jesus a gift too.
Tell him you love him!

163

An angel told Joseph that Jesus wasn't safe in Bethlehem. Egypt was a safe place for Jesus. So Joseph, Mary, and Jesus left for Egypt while it was still dark.

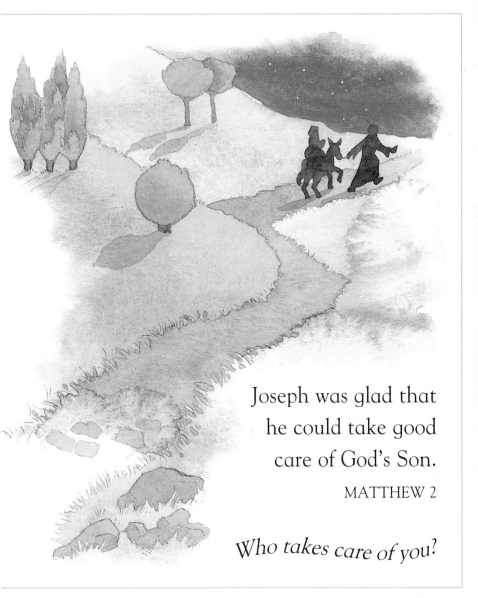

Joseph was glad that
he could take good
care of God's Son.

MATTHEW 2

Who *takes care of you?*

God sent an angel to Joseph.
The angel told him it was
safe to take Jesus home.

Joseph took his family out of Egypt.
They went to live in the town of
Nazareth. Jesus became a strong
and wise boy. He loved his parents,
and they loved him.

MATTHEW 2, LUKE 2

*Ask God to help you grow strong and wise.*

Jesus went to the temple with his family when he was twelve.

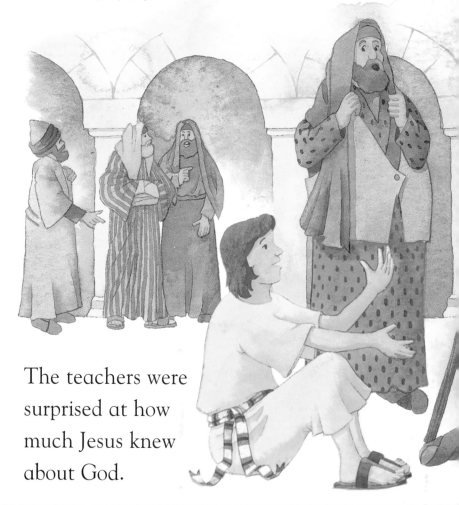

The teachers were surprised at how much Jesus knew about God.

They didn't know that Jesus was God's Son. No wonder he knew so much about God!

LUKE 2

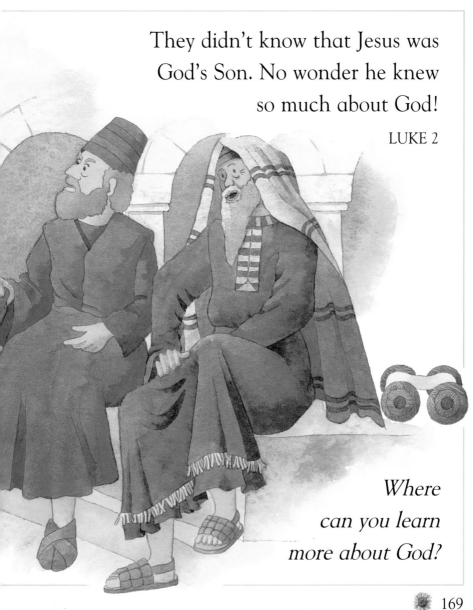

*Where can you learn more about God?*

John the Baptist was Jesus' cousin.

When Jesus grew up, he asked John to baptize him in the Jordan River.

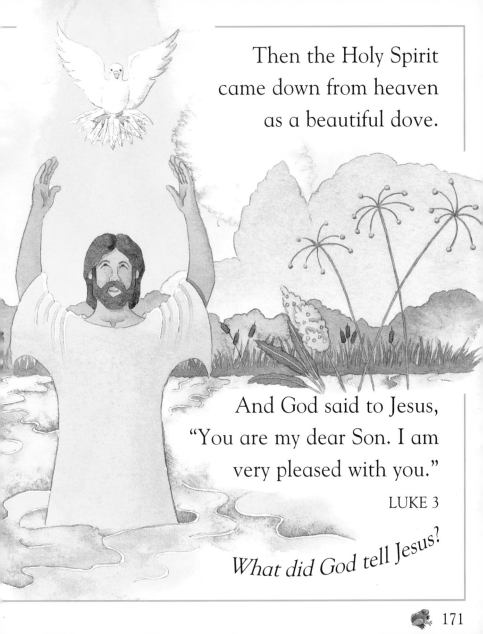

Then the Holy Spirit came down from heaven as a beautiful dove.

And God said to Jesus, "You are my dear Son. I am very pleased with you."

LUKE 3

*What did God tell Jesus?*

171

A man named Nicodemus came
to talk to Jesus one night.

Jesus told Nicodemus that God loved
everyone so much that he even sent
his Son to die for us. Now everyone
who believes in Jesus, God's Son, can
go to heaven someday.

JOHN 3

*How did God show his love for us?*

Jesus chose twelve men to be his disciples.
They went with him everywhere.
They saw him do many miracles,
like making blind people see.

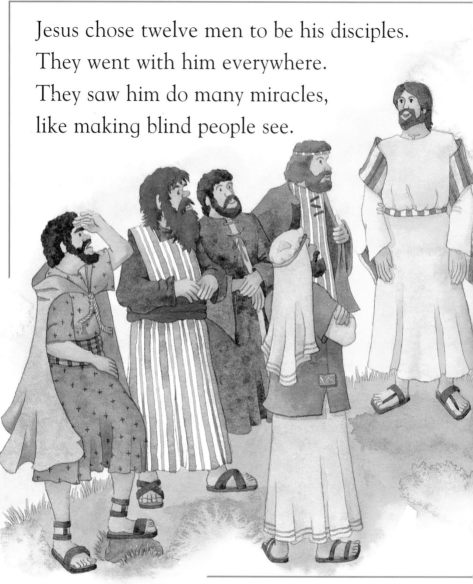

He taught them about God. And he told them about heaven, where he lived before he came to earth. He was their friend. You can be Jesus' friend too.

JOHN 1

Would you like to be Jesus' friend?

Jesus was tired and thirsty from a long walk.
So he asked a woman for some water.

He told her he could give her the kind
of joy that lasts forever. He told her that
God sent him. The woman believed this
and told everyone about Jesus.

JOHN 4

*Do you love Jesus?*
*Then your joy will last forever too!*

Jesus got into a boat
with some fishermen.
They had been fishing all
night without catching
anything.

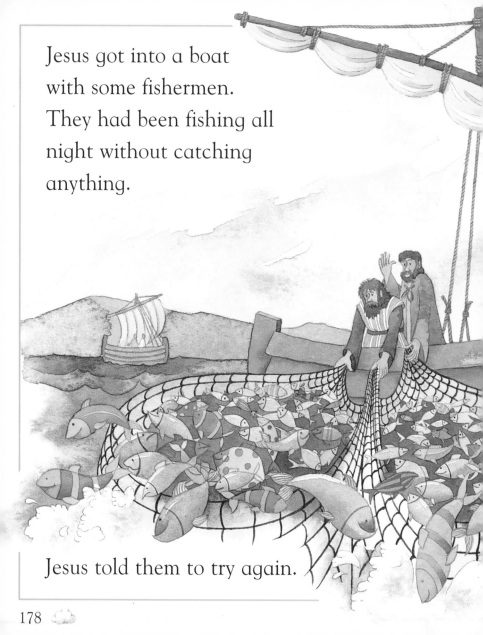

Jesus told them to try again.

The men listened to Jesus, and they caught more fish than their nets could hold! The fishermen were very surprised. They decided to follow Jesus.

LUKE 5

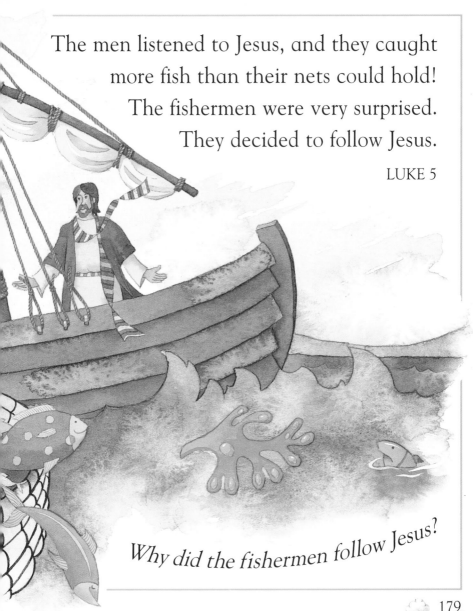

*Why did the fishermen follow Jesus?*

Jesus was teaching a large crowd. Four men wanted Jesus to help a friend who couldn't walk.

So they lowered him through the roof.

They set him down in front of Jesus.

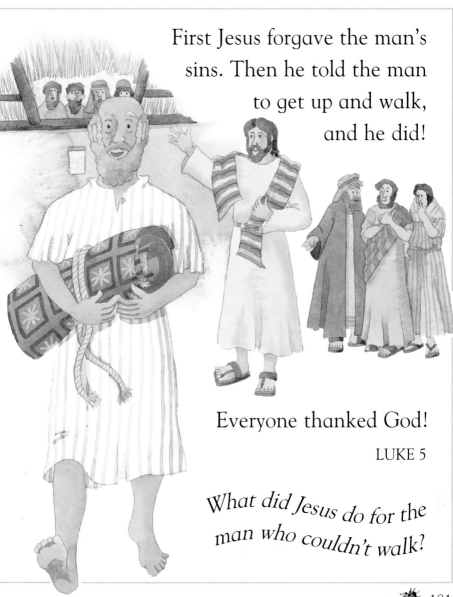

First Jesus forgave the man's sins. Then he told the man to get up and walk, and he did!

Everyone thanked God!

LUKE 5

What did Jesus do for the man who couldn't walk?

181

Another man had been sick for a long time. Jesus asked him if he would like to get well.

The man said, "Yes!" So Jesus told him, "Stand up and walk." Suddenly the man was able to get up and walk!

JOHN 5

*How did the man get well?*

One day Jesus sat down on the side of a mountain.

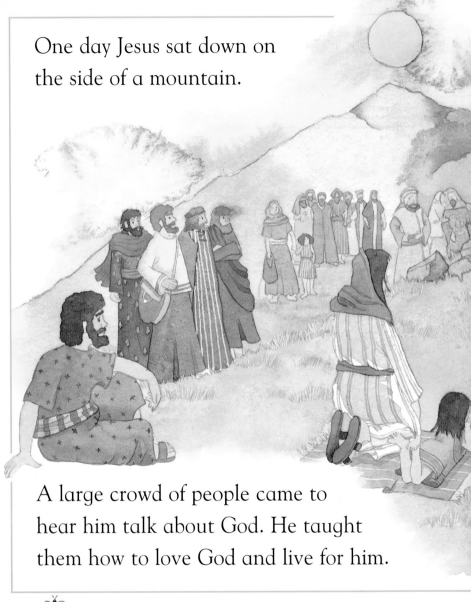

A large crowd of people came to hear him talk about God. He taught them how to love God and live for him.

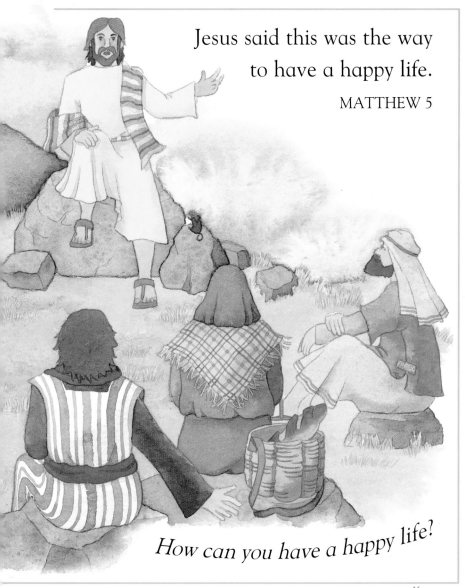

Jesus said this was the way
to have a happy life.

MATTHEW 5

*How can you have a happy life?*

A Roman soldier asked Jesus to heal his servant, who was very sick.

Jesus said he would come to the soldier's house. But the soldier believed that Jesus could stay where he was and just say "Be healed."

So Jesus did. And the servant got well
as soon as Jesus said this!

MATTHEW 8

*What did the soldier believe Jesus could do?*

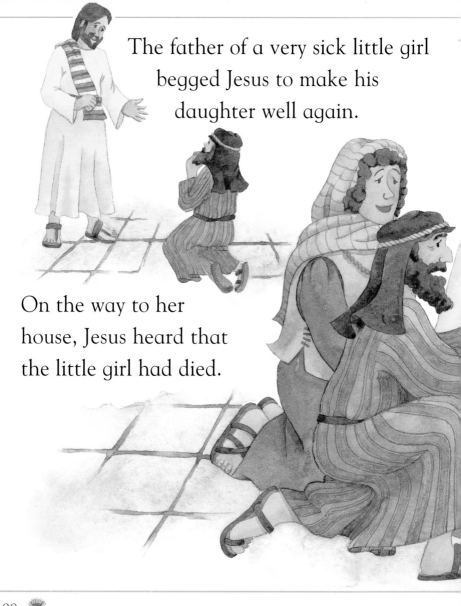

The father of a very sick little girl begged Jesus to make his daughter well again.

On the way to her house, Jesus heard that the little girl had died.

Jesus went to her house anyway. He said, "Get up, my child!" The little girl stood up. She was alive and well again!

LUKE 8

*What did Jesus do for a little girl who died?*

189

This man was blind.
He couldn't see anything.

His friends brought him to Jesus.
They asked Jesus to touch the man
and heal him. Jesus put his hands
on the man's eyes. Suddenly he
could see everything clearly!

MARK 8

*What did the blind man's friends do for him?*

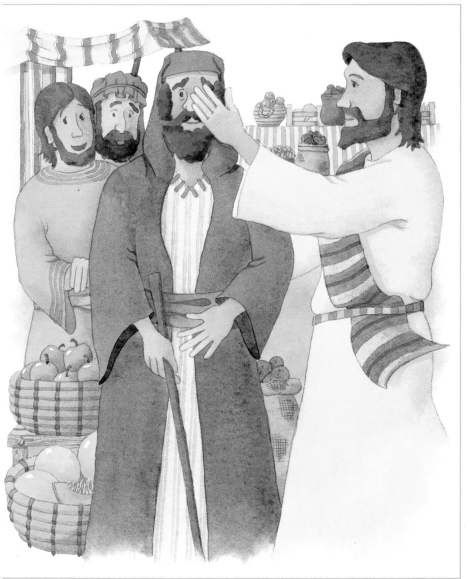

Look at the big waves!

The disciples' small boat
was about to sink. Jesus was quietly sleeping
in the boat. "Wake up!" his disciples yelled.
They were afraid.

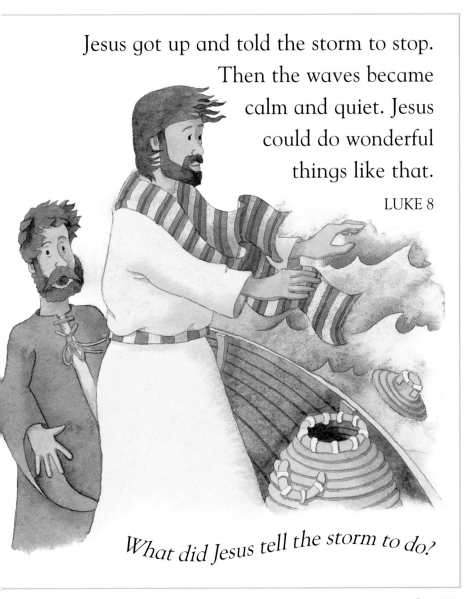

Jesus got up and told the storm to stop. Then the waves became calm and quiet. Jesus could do wonderful things like that.

LUKE 8

*What did Jesus tell the storm to do?*

Did you ever try to walk on water?
Of course not! But Jesus did.

One night the disciples were crossing
the lake in their boat. Suddenly they saw
Jesus walking toward them on the water.

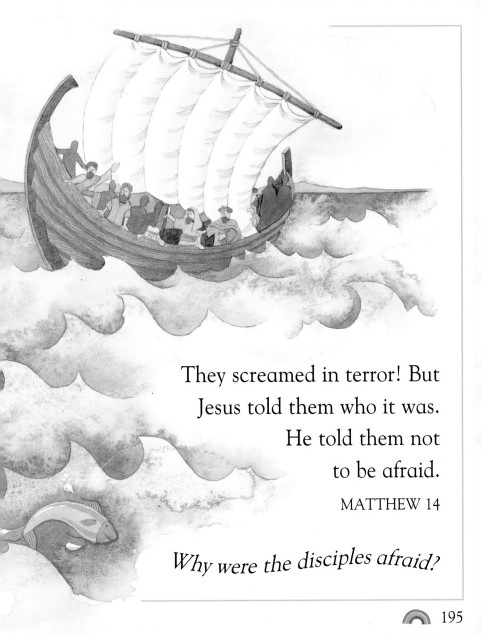

They screamed in terror! But
Jesus told them who it was.
He told them not
to be afraid.

MATTHEW 14

*Why were the disciples afraid?*

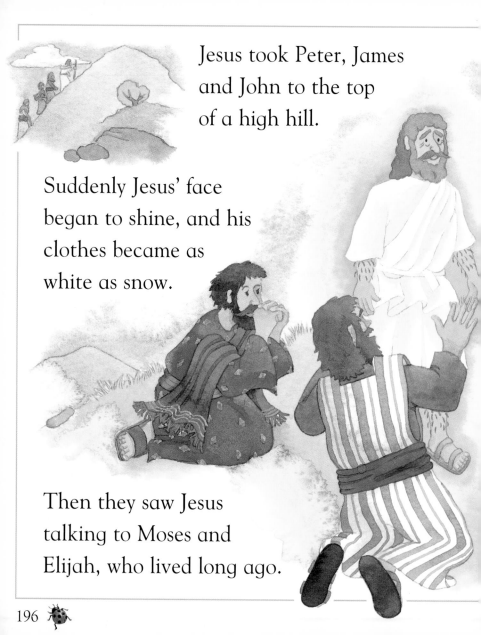

Jesus took Peter, James and John to the top of a high hill.

Suddenly Jesus' face began to shine, and his clothes became as white as snow.

Then they saw Jesus talking to Moses and Elijah, who lived long ago.

And a voice from a bright cloud said, "Jesus is my much loved Son. Listen to him."

MATTHEW 17

*What did the voice from heaven say?*

A big crowd of people followed Jesus.
When they got hungry there were no
stores to buy food.

A boy gave his
lunch of five pieces
of bread and two
fish to Jesus.

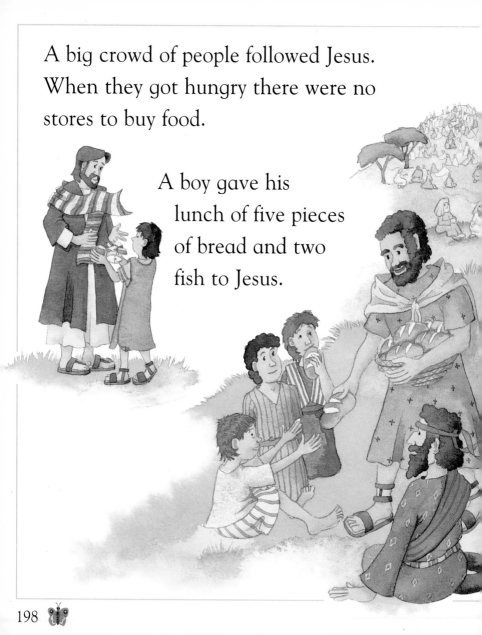

Then Jesus made the bread and fish
become thousands of pieces.
Everybody had enough to eat.
There were even leftovers!

JOHN 6

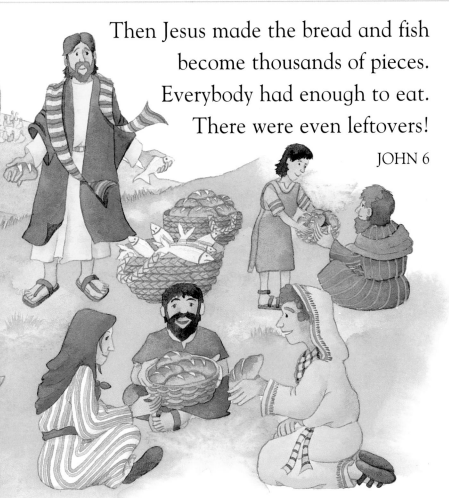

*The boy gave his lunch to Jesus.*
*Can you think of something you can give Jesus?*

A woman whose husband died had only two pennies. Instead of buying something to eat, she put them in the church collection box.

She did this because she loved God. Jesus said she gave more than the rich men who put in many dollars. She put in all she had. But the rich men gave God only a tiny part of their money.

LUKE 21

*What can you give God to show him you love him?*

Some mothers brought their little children to Jesus. They wanted him to touch and bless them. Jesus' disciples told the mothers not to bother Jesus.

But Jesus loved children. He called them to come to him. Jesus said children can believe in him and love him even when they are little.

LUKE 18

*Do you love Jesus?*

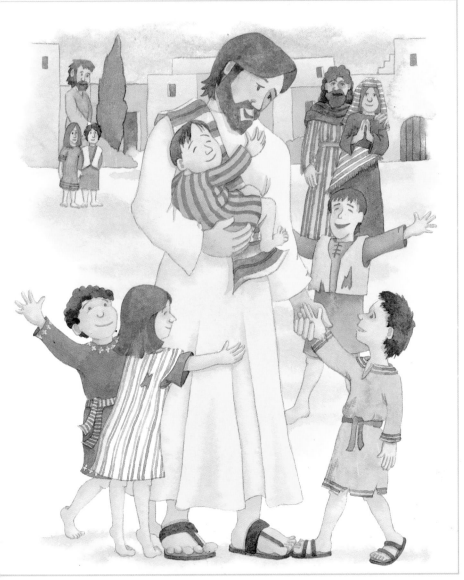

This man was hurt by men who stole his money. They left him in the ditch half dead.

A man he didn't like saw him there. This man put bandages on his cuts. Then he put the man on his donkey and took him to town.

He took care of him. We call the man who helped him the Good Samaritan.

LUKE 10

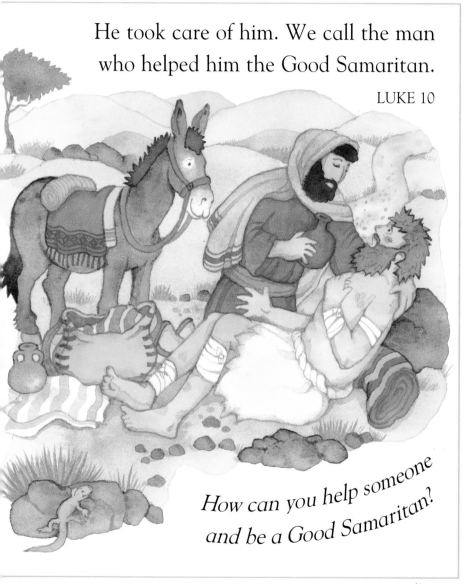

*How can you help someone and be a Good Samaritan?*

Jesus liked to visit two sisters,
Mary and Martha.

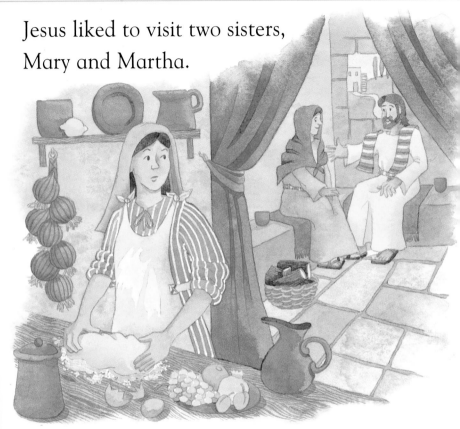

Martha worked hard in the kitchen making
dinner for Jesus. Mary just wanted to talk
with him and learn more about God.
Martha scolded Mary for not helping her.

But Jesus said Mary was doing the
right thing by listening to him.
We listen to Jesus when we
read the Bible.

LUKE 10

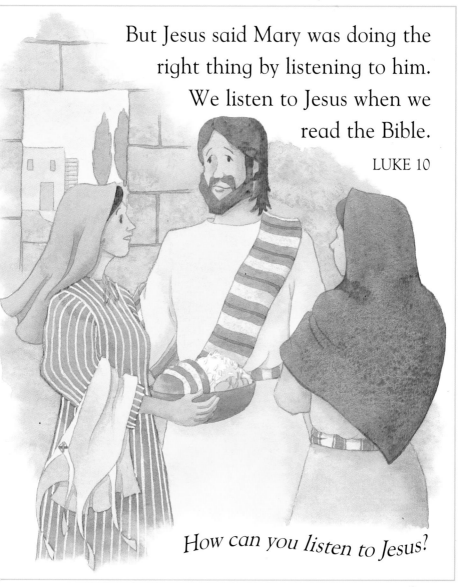

How can you listen to Jesus?

A shepherd takes good care
of his sheep night and day.

Jesus said we are his sheep.
And he cares for us all the time.
He is the Good Shepherd who
knows the names of all his sheep.
You are a little lamb and Jesus
knows your name.

JOHN 10

*Why is Jesus a good shepherd?*

Mary and Martha had a
brother named Lazarus.
Lazarus got sick and died.

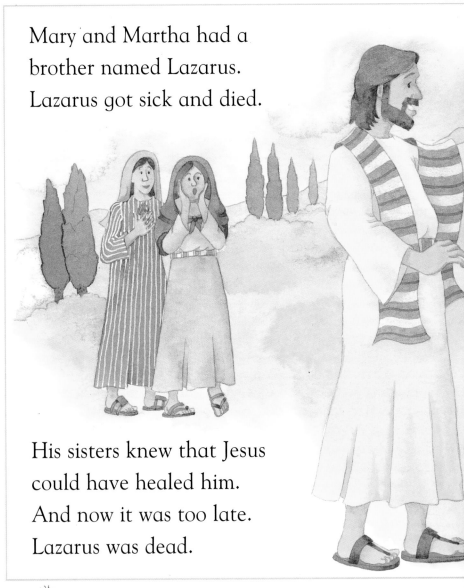

His sisters knew that Jesus
could have healed him.
And now it was too late.
Lazarus was dead.

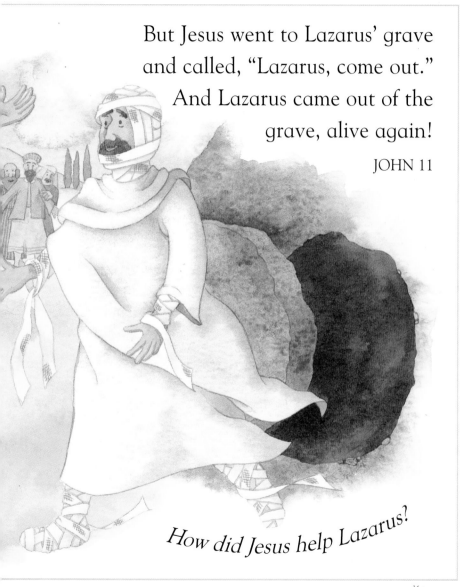

But Jesus went to Lazarus' grave
and called, "Lazarus, come out."
And Lazarus came out of the
grave, alive again!

JOHN 11

*How did Jesus help Lazarus?*

Ten men with bad sores asked
Jesus to make them well.

Jesus told them to go and
show their pastor that the
sores had gone away.

As they went, they suddenly got well again!

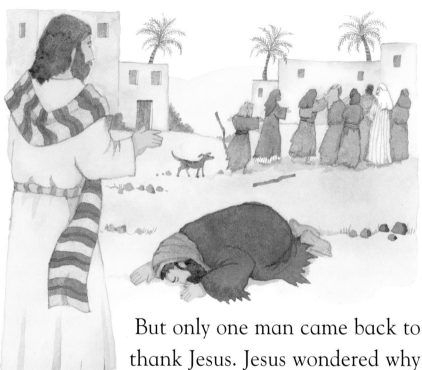

But only one man came back to thank Jesus. Jesus wondered why the other men didn't thank him.

LUKE 17

*What can you thank Jesus for today?*

A man had two sons. The younger son asked his father for a lot of money.

Then the son moved far away.
He did bad things. Soon he ran out
of money. He went home to tell his
father, "I was wrong." His father was
waiting for him and ran to meet him.
He gave his son a big hug!

LUKE 15

*How did the father show his son*
*that he still loved him?*

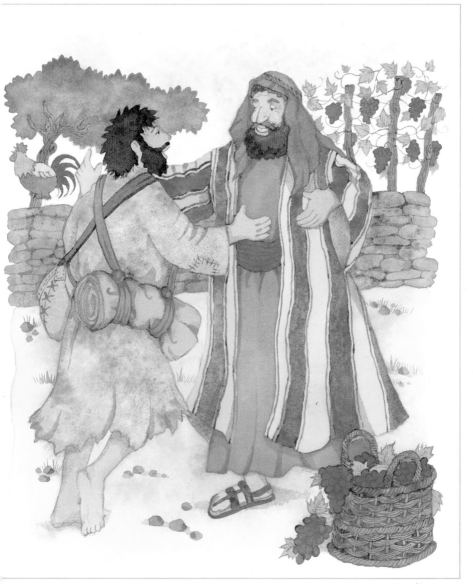

People didn't like Zacchaeus. He cheated them out of their money. But Zacchaeus wanted to see Jesus.

He was too short to see over the crowd, so he climbed a tree.

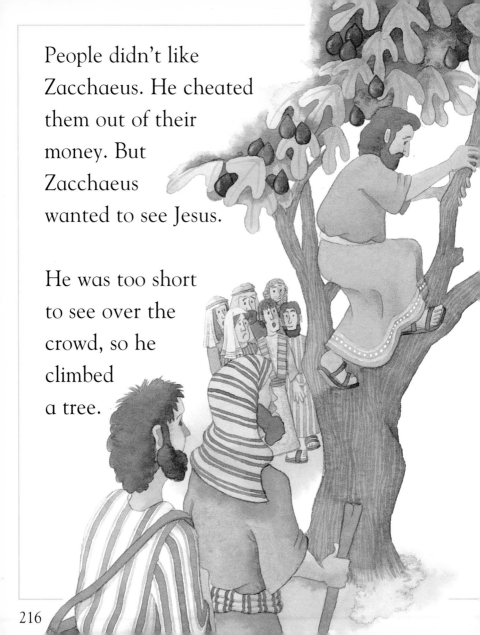

When Jesus walked by, he looked up and told Zacchaeus, "I'm coming to your house."

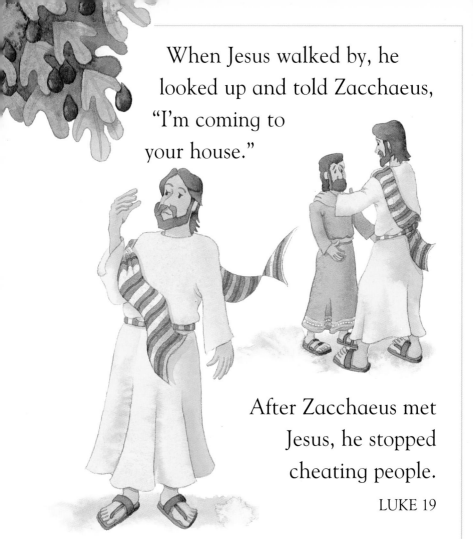

After Zacchaeus met Jesus, he stopped cheating people.

LUKE 19

What did Jesus tell Zacchaeus?

One day Jesus rode a donkey
into Jerusalem.

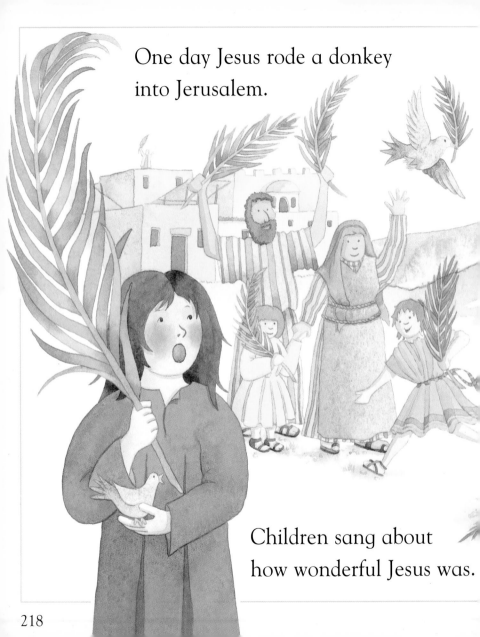

Children sang about
how wonderful Jesus was.

Many people waved palm branches.
They thanked God for Jesus. They
wanted Jesus to be their new king. LUKE 19

*Tell God how wonderful Jesus is!*

One night during supper, Jesus told his disciples it was the last meal he would eat with them on earth.

He knew soldiers would take him away that night, and they would kill him.

Jesus died for you and me, so that God
can forgive us for the bad things we do.

LUKE 22

*Why was this the last meal Jesus
would eat on earth with his disciples?*

After supper Jesus took his
disciples to a garden to pray.
Jesus felt very sad.

He knew the soldiers were coming
soon. He knelt down and prayed
for God to help him. His disciples
were no help—they all fell asleep!
But God sent an angel to make
Jesus strong and brave.

LUKE 22

*Why did God send an angel to Jesus?*

Judas was one of Jesus' disciples, but he only pretended to love Jesus. Some leaders gave Judas money to tell them where to find Jesus.

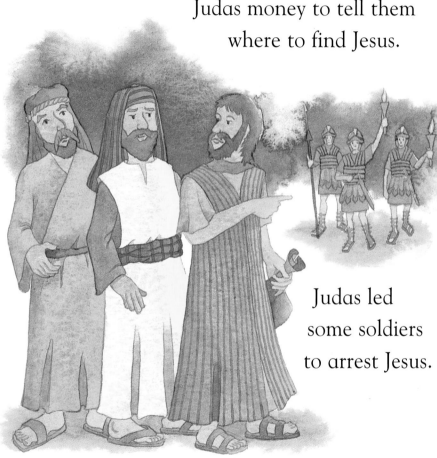

Judas led some soldiers to arrest Jesus.

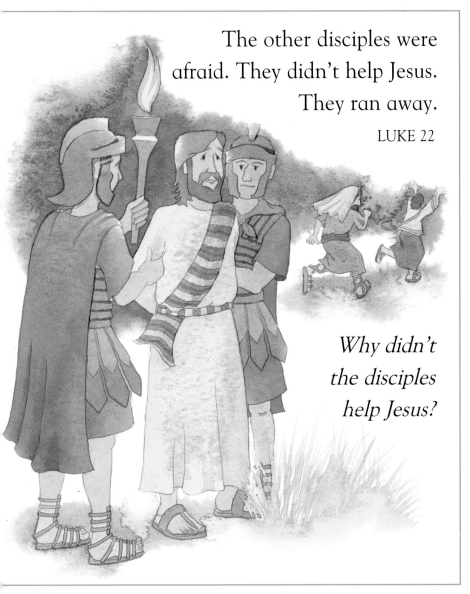

The other disciples were
afraid. They didn't help Jesus.
They ran away.

LUKE 22

*Why didn't
the disciples
help Jesus?*

Peter was one of Jesus' disciples.
He was afraid of the soldiers who
took Jesus away. So he told three
people, "I don't know Jesus!"

Later Peter was sorry he lied.
Jesus forgave him.
After that, Peter wanted to
tell everyone about Jesus!

LUKE 22

*How did Peter feel after he lied?*
*What did Jesus do then?*

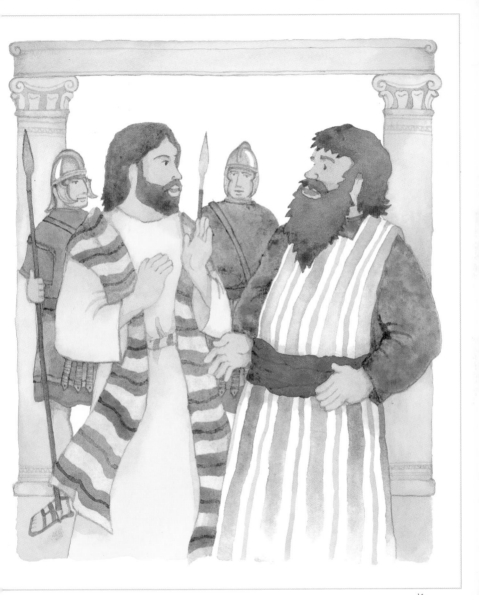

The soldiers took Jesus
to a judge named Pilate.

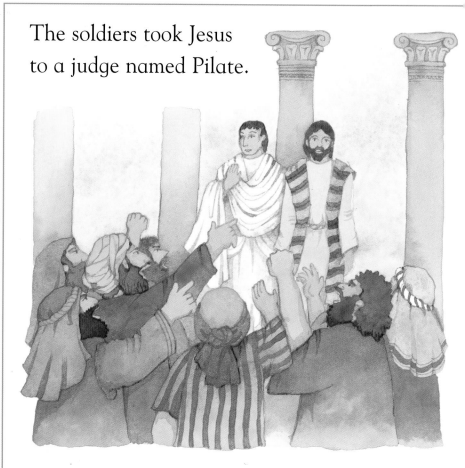

Pilate decided Jesus hadn't done anything
wrong. He wanted to let him go. But the
people kept yelling, "Kill him, Kill him!"

They shouted louder and louder
until Pilate said the soldiers
could do this terrible thing.

LUKE 23

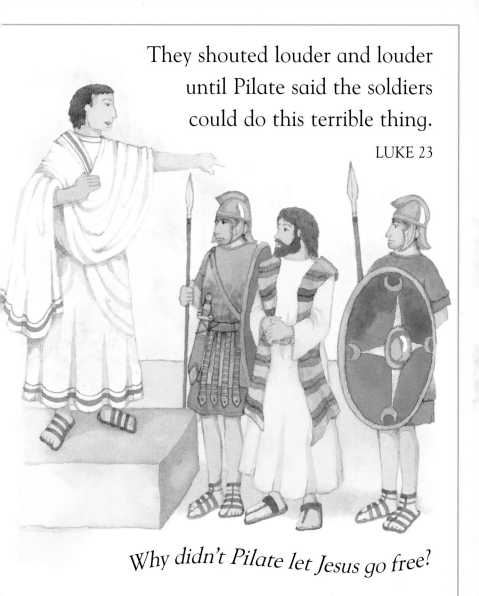

Why *didn't Pilate let Jesus go free?*

The soldiers nailed Jesus
to a cross made of wood.
They put two bad
men on crosses
next to him.

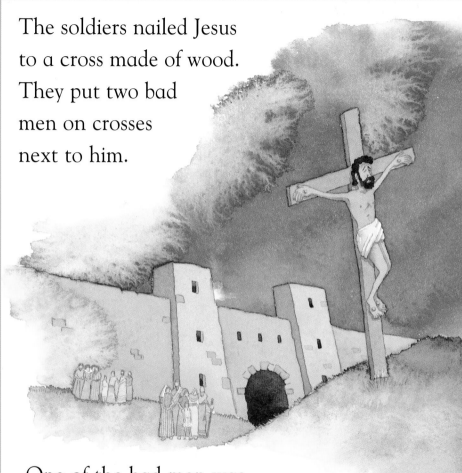

One of the bad men was
sorry for his sins. He asked Jesus to
forgive him. Jesus said yes, he would do that.

Jesus forgives everyone
who asks him to.
He will forgive you.

LUKE 23

*What must we do if we want Jesus to forgive us?*

After Jesus was dead, some friends put his body in a cave.

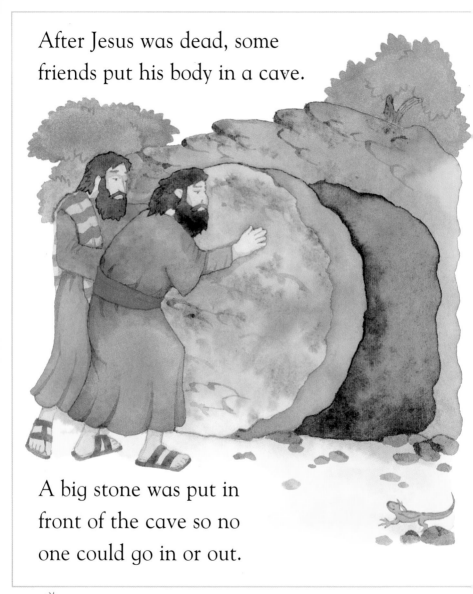

A big stone was put in front of the cave so no one could go in or out.

But early on Sunday morning Jesus came back to life and came out of the grave! He was alive again!

LUKE 24

*Did Jesus stay in the cave?*

Jesus' friends could hardly believe that he was alive again. So he showed them the nail marks in his hands and feet.

One day he rose up into the sky and disappeared in a cloud! He went back to his Father in heaven. Someday he will come back to earth again!

LUKE 24, ACTS 1

*Where did Jesus go?*

After Jesus had gone to heaven,
his friends had a big meeting.
Suddenly there was a
loud noise!

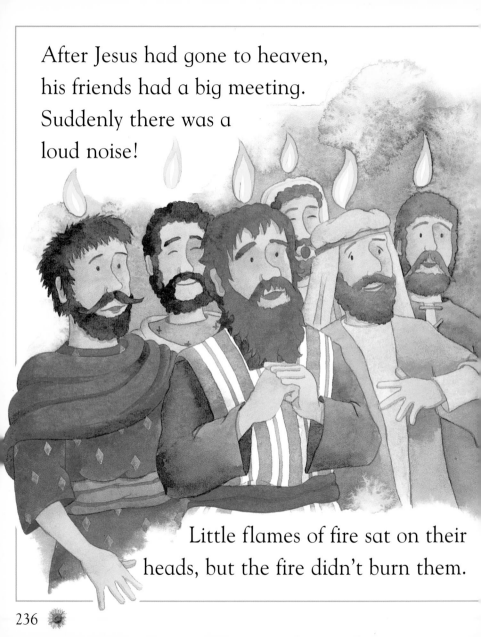

Little flames of fire sat on their
heads, but the fire didn't burn them.

God's Holy Spirit came to live in their hearts.
The Holy Spirit helps us believe in Jesus.

ACTS 2

*Who came to live in the hearts of Jesus' friends?*

Paul didn't believe that Jesus was God's son. He even tried to kill people who believed in Jesus.

One day a bright light blinded him, and he fell down.

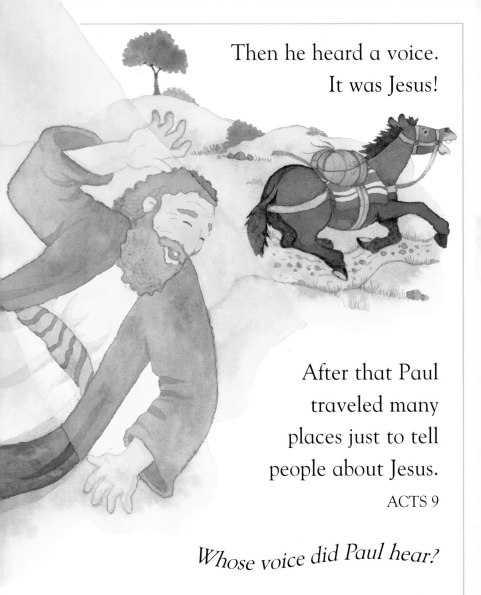

Then he heard a voice.
It was Jesus!

After that Paul
traveled many
places just to tell
people about Jesus.
ACTS 9

*Whose voice did Paul hear?*

239

Many people believed in Jesus when they heard Paul preach in Damascus.

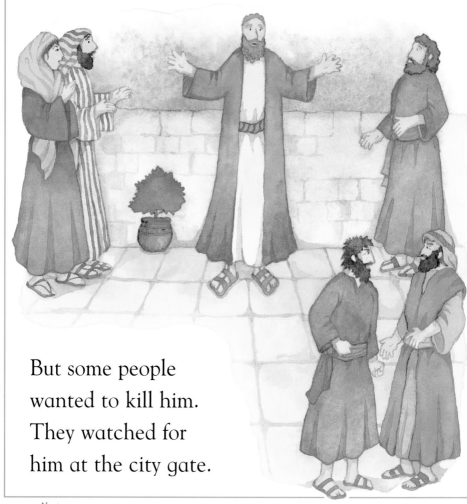

But some people wanted to kill him. They watched for him at the city gate.

Paul's friends put him in a big basket. Then they lowered him to the ground through a hole in the wall. He was safe!

ACTS 9

*How did Paul's friends help him?*

A man named Cornelius wanted
to know more about God.

So an angel told
Cornelius where
to find Peter.

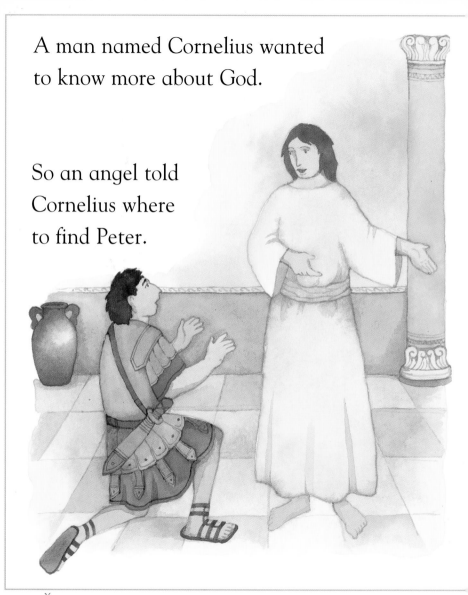

Cornelius sent two of his servants
to invite Peter to visit him.

Then Peter told Cornelius and his friends
how Jesus could forgive their sins.

ACTS 10

*What did Peter tell Cornelius?*

243

"Stop telling people about Jesus!"
the soldiers said to Peter.
But Peter wouldn't stop.

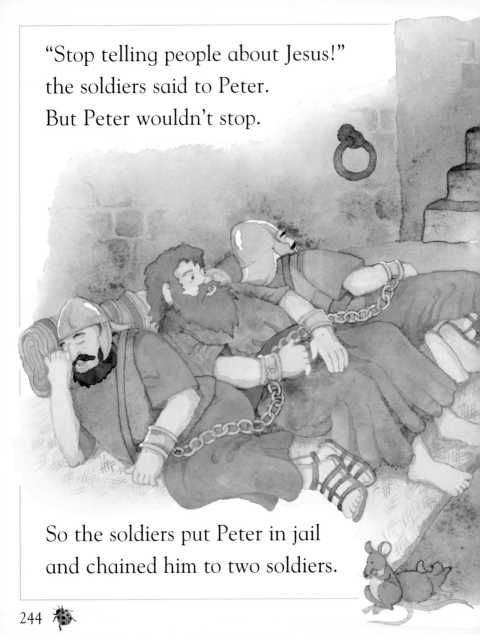

So the soldiers put Peter in jail
and chained him to two soldiers.

But that night an angel came and told Peter, "Come with me!"

Peter's chains fell off, and the prison doors opened. Peter was free!

ACTS 12

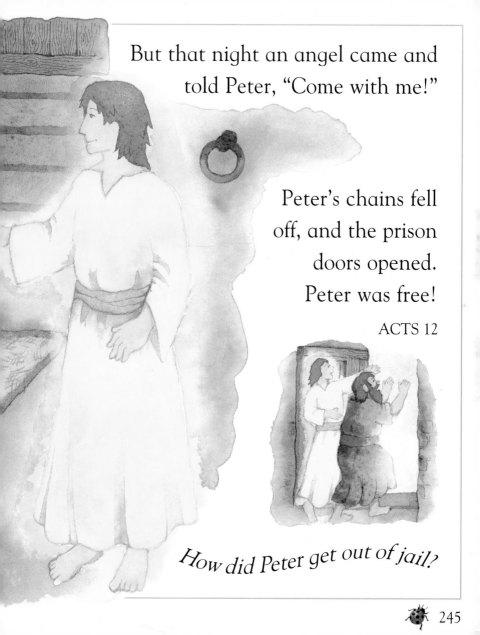

How did Peter get out of jail?

Timothy's mother and
grandmother loved God.

They knew that Jesus loved them
and died on the cross so that God
could forgive their sins. They
taught Timothy these things when
he was very young, and he gave
his life to Jesus. Timothy told God
he would always obey him.

2 TIMOTHY 1

*Who taught Timothy about Jesus?*

Paul met with a group of women who were praying by the banks of a river.

He told them all about Jesus being God's Son.

One of the women was Lydia. She believed in God, but had never heard of Jesus.

After she listened to Paul, Lydia believed in Jesus, too.

ACTS 16

How did Lydia hear about Jesus?

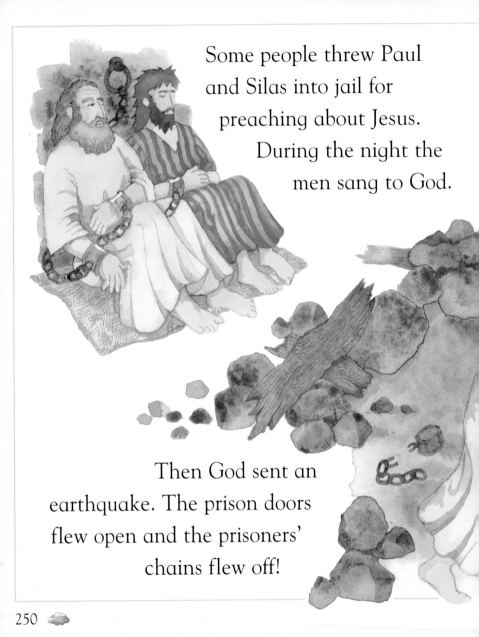

Some people threw Paul
and Silas into jail for
preaching about Jesus.
During the night the
men sang to God.

Then God sent an
earthquake. The prison doors
flew open and the prisoners'
chains flew off!

The jailer was afraid.
Paul told him and his
family about Jesus. Then
they all believed in Jesus!

ACTS 16

*What happened after the earthquake?*

Paul met a husband
and wife, Aquila
and Priscilla.

They made tents for
a living. Paul made
tents too.

He taught them all
about Jesus, God's Son.
And they believed
in Jesus.

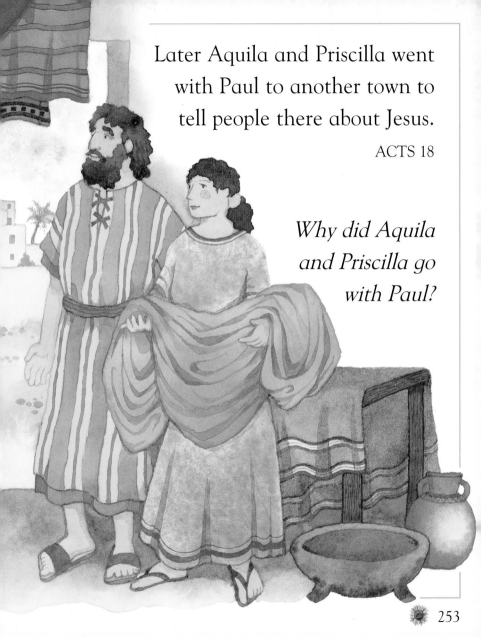

Later Aquila and Priscilla went with Paul to another town to tell people there about Jesus.

ACTS 18

*Why did Aquila and Priscilla go with Paul?*

253

John had been one of Jesus' best friends. When John was very old, Jesus came to him in a vision. Jesus told John about things that will happen.

The best thing is this: Jesus will come back someday! Then everyone who believes in Jesus will live with him forever in heaven.

REVELATION 1

*What was the best thing Jesus told John?*

Kenneth N. Taylor is best known as the creator of *The Living Bible*, which sold over 40 million copies. That Bible has now been revised by a group of biblical scholars to become the New Living Translation.

In June 2005 Kenneth Taylor went home to be with the Savior he loved. He is survived by his wife, Margaret, ten grown children, 28 grandchildren, and more than 20 great-grandchildren, so he personally told many children about God!

Through his children's books, Dr. Taylor continues to share the gospel with boys and girls today. Some of his most loved books include *Big Thoughts for Little People*, *The Bible in Pictures for Little Eyes*, and *Everything a Child Should Know about God*.